Praise for *Longshot*

"Zach captures the energy, spirit, and sheer fun of building one of the most unique political phenomena in modern American politics. This book is a harbinger of the meta-political changes for generations to come and is an absolute must read."

—Saagar Enjeti, co-host of *Breaking Points*

"Zach took an unknown candidate and made him into the most improbable of household names. The Yang campaign created a die-hard group of supporters, leveraged alternative media, and built a movement. *Longshot* is a candid, entertaining, and informative look behind the scenes at how they were able to accomplish that."

—Lis Smith, Senior Communications Director, Pete Buttigieg

"The prospect of Universal Basic Income as inevitable U.S. policy would not be where it is today without the 21st century tactics laid out in *Longshot*. Zach was an integral part of getting the country to know the name 'Andrew Yang' against all efforts made by the traditional political/media machine to ignore and minimize his presidential campaign."

—Scott Santens, Universal Basic Income advocate

LONGSHOT

LONGSHOT

How Political Nobodies Took Andrew Yang

National—and the New Playbook That

Let Us Build a Movement

ZACH GRAUMANN

BenBella Books, Inc.
Dallas, TX

BenBella Books, Inc.
10440 N. Central Expressway
Suite 800
Dallas, TX 75231
benbellabooks.com
Send feedback to feedback@benbellabooks.com

BenBella is a federally registered trademark.

Printed in the United States of America
10 9 8 7 6 5 4 3 2 1

Library of Congress Control Number: 2021953528
ISBN 9781637740385
eISBN 9781637740392

Editing by Alexa Stevenson and Alyn Wallace
Copyediting by Scott Calamar
Proofreading by Sarah Vostok and Jenny Bridges
Indexing by Amy Murphy
Text design and composition by PerfecType, Nashville, TN
Cover design by Sarah Avinger
Cover photography by Marc Klockow
Printed by Lake Book Manufacturing

For the Yang Gang—this campaign was, is, and always will be, yours.

CONTENTS

"When you're young, you think the cavalry is coming to save us. When you grow up, you realize that you are the cavalry."

—Andrew Yang

INTRODUCTION

"How about now?" Frawley shouted from across the room. Andrew Frawley—who lost his first name to the campaign (can't have two Andrews on the Andrew Yang campaign)—was a six-foot-five, two-hundred-plus-pound giant with messy brown hair, a youthful glow, and, at the moment, a precarious perch atop a wheeled desk chair.

Preventing Frawley from being dumped unceremoniously onto the floor was our head of operations, Muhan Zhang, a slight twenty-seven-year-old with a much lower center of gravity; he struggled to keep the chair from rolling away while Frawley stood fully stretched to hang the wrinkled YANG 2020 banner that would serve as part of the backdrop for that night's event.

It was August 1, 2018, and we were preparing the newly opened Friends of Andrew Yang campaign headquarters in Manhattan for one of our first public campaign events. As much as we griped about the location—way too close to the tourist traffic of Times Square—there was no denying it was convenient. Not only did its proximity to NYC's main train stations make it an easy commute for every member of our five-person staff, but it was also close enough for Andrew to bike there from his apartment in Hell's Kitchen.

Andrew Yang was a successful entrepreneur and nonprofit executive, but at that point he was also virtually unknown. He had built and led a popular education tech company, Manhattan Prep, sold it for a small fortune, and used his earnings to launch his most recent social enterprise, Venture for America (aimed at helping recent college grads create businesses in economically stressed cities), which had gotten him named a "Presidential Ambassador for Entrepreneurship" by President Obama back in 2015. But despite his impressive résumé, the American public couldn't have picked Andrew out of a lineup. He had no particular following, on social media or elsewhere. He had no email list, donor base, or network of political connections. He had never held elected office of any kind, and he possessed no governing experience whatsoever. And yet he was, against the advice of essentially everyone, running for president of the United States of America.

Naturally, the staff he'd been able to assemble weren't exactly seasoned political professionals. Our campaign team consisted of a recent Virginia Commonwealth University graduate with a marketing degree (Frawley), a tech generalist who'd worked for Andrew at Venture for America (Muhan), and three people I haven't introduced yet: a former hedge-fund analyst, a former LSAT teacher, and an ex–Wall Street executive/founder of a small nonprofit (Carly Reilly, Matt Shinners, and me, respectively). Matt was the oldest, at thirty-four, and our team's combined years of political experience totaled exactly zero.

But what we lacked in experience . . . we also lacked in funding. At the time of this particular event, the campaign had less than $75,000 in the bank. While this sounds like a decent amount of money (hey, it's more than most of us make in a year), for context, Senators Elizabeth Warren and Kamala Harris—neither of whom had even officially announced their candidacy at this point—were rumored to have stocked up nearly $10 million in their war chests. Each. To start—keyword *start*—their presidential runs. They were also expected to raise upward of $50 million—again, *each*—before the 2020 Iowa caucus, which was then just over a year away. Our $75,000 was barely enough to pay for that month's rent/payroll/ expenses; never mind the year until Iowa, we were operating on a month-to-month basis, just scratching and fighting for our continued existence.

These obvious facts did not seem to faze our young team. In fact, spirits had never been higher—probably because, until recently, we'd been operating out of Andrew's mom's one-bedroom apartment (where Muhan was also living).

"Frawley—move it two inches higher," I shouted from the back of the room. Our new headquarters was a classic garment-district warehouse turned corporate office, a single cavernous space with twenty-foot ceilings and massive windows along one wall of the unit. The room was full of shitty IKEA furniture because none of us had any idea how to furnish an office (and no real money to do it even if we had). The hardwood floors were always covered in a thin layer of nasty old-NYC-building dust, despite our best attempts with the Swiffer, and the space was either too hot (in the summer) or too cold (in the winter)—no in-between.

It's worth emphasizing how ridiculous this office looked. "Decorate the office" was low on our priority list, and responsibility for the task was split between Muhan, Frawley, and myself. The result was, well, exactly what you would expect from three dudes decorating an office—painfully white walls with nothing on them except a scattering of campaign signs and paraphernalia haphazardly hung with Scotch tape, a couple of Andrew Yang street-art posters made by some of our early (and rare) fans, our Wi-Fi password handwritten on a piece of notebook paper, and a few Michael Scott quotes I'd scribbled in Sharpie onto white printer paper and stuck up for inspiration. The banner Frawley was hanging was new, and had probably looked good at one point, but we had stupidly rolled it up and tossed it in a corner somewhere when it arrived, so it was now being hung on the wall looking like it used to wave off the back of someone's truck. Right next to it was the biggest sign in the room, a three-by-two-foot poster I'd had made at Kinko's and hung on one of the very first days in our new campaign HQ:

"Andrew Yang is a longer-than-long-shot for the White House."

The New York Times

*February 10, 2018**

On one hand, I hated that quote. *Screw you,* New York Times! *Three weeks before the 2016 election you said Hillary Clinton had a 91 percent chance of winning! Your paper sucks!*

On the other hand, I loved it. *Our candidate was covered by THE* New York Times*! You're by definition not such a longshot if the* New York Times *is talking about you!*

Either way, it was great motivation. The *New York Times* doesn't think we can win? *Let's prove them wrong.*

Andrew arrived right as the event started (on his bike, of course, which we stored in a far corner of the office) and greeted everyone as they walked in. By 7 PM, a whopping eighteen people (a few of whom Andrew already knew) had

---

* The actual quote was: "That candidate is Andrew Yang, a well-connected New York business-man who is mounting a longer-than-long-shot bid for the White House." But that didn't look as good on a sign.

arrived to hear our candidate outline his vision for the country. They drank some of the discount Stella Artois beers we'd bought at the CVS next door, and snacked on the Tostitos Hint of Lime chips we'd arranged (still in the original bags, of course) on plastic foldout tables we'd ordered from Amazon. Naturally, we'd forgotten to buy napkins, so we'd set out a roll of paper towels, which guests tore off as needed. If you were dubious about Andrew's chances before you arrived, our event-planning expertise definitely wasn't changing your mind.

After thirty or forty minutes of mingling, I officially welcomed everyone and gave Andrew's introduction, and he took his place in front of the wrinkled YANG 2020 banner, illuminated by IKEA lamps. Absolutely nothing about our makeshift setup looked remotely presidential.

His appearance didn't help. Andrew's hair was . . . an experience. It looked like a child had cut it (and not a particularly talented child). Never combed, it stuck out in multiple directions and was flat in all the wrong places. He wore a pair of too-baggy and too-long Levi's, an overwashed light-blue button-down with a droopy collar, and a pair of never-polished brown dress shoes scuffed from years of wear. He'd topped this ensemble off with a blue suit jacket (not a blazer—literally the jacket half of a business suit), and pinned to his left lapel was a big white campaign button featuring the "Yang Y" logo, which Business Insider would later call "an abomination."* The overall effect was less "potential world leader" and more "engineering professor/Silicon Valley wonk about to give a TED Talk."

And in fact, this wasn't far off. His stump speech at that point basically *was* a TED Talk. It began with some terrifying statistics about how automation is going to eliminate millions of American jobs and how woefully unprepared our country is to handle this, and then he presented the core of his solution: universal basic income (UBI, for short—essentially, under Andrew's plan, giving every American adult $1,000 a month). He explained his flagship UBI proposal in convincing

---

* The logo predated our team—Andrew had a friend do it and guided the creative himself. Unfortunately, this kind of thing wasn't exactly Andrew's strength (see "Venture for America," a name literally created by changing one word of "Teach for America"). The "abomination" quote came when Business Insider eventually did a feature on all of the candidates' logos and brands and ranked ours dead last. So yes, the visual representation of our extremely unique candidate was an extremely basic red-white-and-blue color scheme with a weird Y that sort of looked like a bird . . . and we were rolling with it.

detail, then touched on "Medicare for All," laying out a unique business argument for the government providing health care, along with how we might make it happen. He didn't use slides that night, but only because I told him we couldn't get the projector to work (not entirely true, but I felt like presidential candidates shouldn't be breaking out PowerPoint decks—a version of a fight we would have in various ways throughout the campaign).

TED Talk or not, his stump speech was compelling. It was very matter-of-fact, specific, and logical, and his speaking style was fairly monotone. That said, he had natural wit and a subtle straight-faced humor, and his genuineness shone through, especially as he moved into his strongest argument—that the way we measure the economy (GDP, stock-market growth) is fundamentally flawed, and that we should be building a more "human-centered economy" that measures and incentivizes the things that really tell us how we're doing, like life expectancy, happiness, childhood education levels, and so on.

Something about the way Andrew laid out information made you trust that he was right, and you could feel a slow but tangible shift in the audience as he spoke: *Holy shit, maybe he's not that crazy.* People stopped cocking their heads skeptically and actually started nodding; you could see them starting to believe in Andrew Yang, at least a little. He was no longer a longshot presidential hopeful with no chance of winning, he was a patriotic visionary who wanted to make this country better for all of us, with concrete ideas about how to do it.

Then he started to go sideways.

Despite hours of me, Muhan, and Frawley coaching (read: begging) him not to, Andrew began talking about something he calls "digital social credits" (DSCs)—his solution for the economy and society in a potential future in which virtually all jobs have been wiped out by automation.

"People need more than work to live a fulfilling life," he argued, "so we need to create a new currency where the government gives citizens credit for volunteering, caring for the elderly, and other things that our financial market does not pay for. It'll be like credit card points or a punch card at your local deli—the government administers points that people can accumulate and trade in for other undervalued services."

One donor once told me it's too "beep-boop, beep-boop" for the average person. That's generous. It's an insane talking point for a no-name candidate trying to be taken seriously. For one thing, the idea itself has . . . problems.* For another, we were already far-out enough; throwing in the concept of DSCs brought everyone back to earth and reminded them of just how ridiculous we were. It was like a bubble popped—he lost half the room instantly, and you could see people's expressions change from thoughtful and interested to wondering: *What the fuck is this guy talking about?*

He finally moved on to taking questions, and it's a mark of how exceptional Andrew is at Q&A that he nearly got the audience back to where they were before his digital social credits detour. He really warms up one-on-one, and he can engage with people on almost any topic—he may be the smartest person I've ever met— and the event wrapped with some decent applause.

As the crowd trickled out, the majority had the vibe of people who'd just seen a unique play or lecture—they were curious about what Andrew Yang would do next, while having no expectation of ever casting a ballot in his favor. A few people truly seemed to like him, and three or four guests even hung around to chat with Andrew and were convinced to sign our "campaign wall" (a randomly chosen spot we'd thought it would look cool to have people write on, like a visual demonstration of the support for our campaign).† Frawley had taken a photo of the event, angled to make the crowd look bigger, and we posted it to the official Andrew Yang Instagram and Twitter accounts, which had approximately seven thousand followers combined. I'm confident that, except for us, no one in that photo—hell, no one who liked that post—thought Andrew Yang had a chance of becoming president, or even being considered a serious contender for the role.

I overheard one guest laughing with another on his way out: "Interesting event. That guy has no shot."

---

* Aside from the logistical and ethical nightmare (who assigns the point values?), the name calls up China's "social credit score" system, which has mostly been used to punish citizens for doing things the government doesn't approve of. There's an entire *Black Mirror* episode on Netflix explaining why this idea is terrible.

† It probably would have looked cooler if it hadn't had fewer than one hundred signatures on it—including our own and those of every single person who stepped into the office that we could convince to sign. Andrew's mom, package delivery guys, the landlord, our significant others . . . it was a massive wall, and one hundred signatures filling up 2 percent of the surface area was actually a pretty good reflection of where we were relative to our Herculean goals.

Flash forward just over one year.

It's September 30, 2019. Andrew and the six full-time staffers and two very large security guards that make up his "road team" are huddled in a small greenroom. (By now I've learned that most "greenrooms" aren't actually green—this one is basically a concrete storage closet with a few chairs and too many snacks.) Along with me and Carly, the group includes our traveling press secretary (not to be confused with our other, non–traveling press secretary), our head of advance (a position I hadn't known existed fourteen months ago—basically in charge of planning wherever we'll be next and setting things up . . . in advance), Andrew's "body man" (like Gary from *Veep*; basically a personal assistant who's with him at all times), and a full-time videographer (wielding the kind of massive camera you need a back brace to carry).

From our concrete room behind the outdoor stage, we can hear a roar from the crowd as MC Jin—one of the most famous Asian rappers in America, and our opening act—hypes them up. We are in MacArthur Park in Los Angeles, where a production company has erected a stage complete with concert-quality lighting, sound system, and large and loud pyrotechnics (sparks are literally flying), and where a few thousand people had been waiting since 3 PM. It's now almost 7, and the energy of the crowd seems to shake the walls. MC Jin finishes up, and the audience starts chanting "AN-DREW YANG! AN-DREW YANG! AN-DREW YANG!"

Minutes before, I'd been frustrated.

"What is with this traffic?" I'd complained from the front seat of one of the three giant black SUVs that made up our motorcade—Los Angeles traffic was always bad, but it was bumper to bumper as we got close to the venue.

Then, through the windshield, I saw a group of eight people crossing the street together carrying YANG GANG signs, wearing MATH hats and NOT LEFT, NOT RIGHT, FORWARD T-shirts, and I got it—the traffic was caused by *us*. This was *our* traffic. Andrew Yang traffic.

Now, in our packed not-so-green room, Andrew is picking at his pre-rally snacks of choice.* His hair has clearly been cut by an adult professional, and it is impeccably styled. He wears a custom-tailored navy Havana blazer from Suitsupply,

---

* BelVita crackers, SkinnyPop, and Tate's cookies, in case you're curious.

a freshly pressed light-blue button-down shirt, well-fitting chinos, and polished black dress shoes. The large, white Y button of last year has been replaced with the campaign's signature MATH pin, which we have sold tens of thousands of online. We have just spent the day with Elon Musk and Donald Glover, and our candidate is preparing to take the stage of what amounts to a political rock concert.

When it's time, in true rock-star fashion, Andrew hypes himself up with his own personal routine: He jerks his arms and legs, looks up, and yells "Aaghhh!!" It's sort of "pro-wrestler before entering the ring," or "basketball player after making an 'and one.'" Supposedly, he is imitating Nicolas Cage right before he steals a car in *Gone in 60 Seconds,* but I promise that no one watching would make that connection.

Then:

"Ladies and gentlemen, it is my pleasure to introduce . . . THE NEXT PRESIDENT OF THE UNITED STATES . . . ANNNNNNNDREWWWWW YANG!"

Andrew bursts onto the stage with his arms stretched wide and head back to face the darkened Los Angeles sky; Mark Morrison's "Return of the Mack" starts blasting, and the pyrotechnics pop off golden fireworks on both sides of the stage. The standing-room-only crowd is screaming—some are hoisting giant papier-mâché Yang heads adorned with MATH hats, massive signs bearing Andrew's name or Bitmoji likeness bob up and down, and oversized $1,000 bills printed with Yang's face spin in the air above the sea of supporters.

Over seven thousand people have crammed into MacArthur Park on this warm LA night. It is a noticeably diverse crowd—by age, ethnicity, any way you slice it. But they all have one thing in common: they are fired *up* for Andrew Yang.

Standing in the wings, I make eye contact with Carly across the stage—we are both wearing the same expression, best described as "Jim from *The Office* when he finds out Pam is pregnant": *Can you believe this!? What is happening!?*

Andrew Yang had become a national superstar. He had millions of supporters—we'd gone from a combined seven thousand to a combined three million followers on all platforms. We had just raised $10 million from nearly three hundred thousand *different* people in the third quarter, were on our way to topping $40 million total, and had done it all with donations that averaged thirty-five dollars each.[1] We had nearly one hundred paid staff, and had built an online army—the "Yang Gang"—that numbered in the hundreds of thousands across the country, and seasoned political professionals were asking to work on the campaign. By now, Andrew had been on three Democratic debate stages, headlined *The Late Show with Stephen Colbert*, *The Daily Show*, *Tucker Carlson Tonight*, *The Rachel Maddow Show*, *The View*, and nearly any other national news or news-adjacent show you can think of. He had been profiled by the *New York Times*, the *Washington Post*, *The Atlantic*, *Politico*, BuzzFeed, *Rolling Stone*, and the *Wall Street Journal*, among others. CNN had recently called him "the hottest candidate this side of Elizabeth Warren," and he was polling fifth nationwide in the primary. Somehow, in a historically crowded Democratic field, Andrew Yang had managed to stand out and stay in.

That night, he glided around the firework-lit stage like he had been performing at this level his entire life. He was hamming it up, and kept having to pause while the crowd laughed at his dad jokes—they started an impromptu "POW-ER-POINT" chant after he made a crack about being the first president to use a PowerPoint deck at the State of the Union. After his standard talking point about how the one thing all Democrats want is to beat Donald Trump, and he's beating Trump head-to-head in every poll out there, he went off script:

"It's like a game of rock paper scissors," he crowed to the crowd, "and if Donald Trump is the scissors . . . I'm the fucking rock!"

The crowd went wild. "YANG BEATS TRUMP! YANG BEATS TRUMP! YANG BEATS TRUMP!"

In a movie, this would be the point where a record scratches and you freeze the frame.

How the heck did we get here?

How did we go from poorly attended Tostitos-on-folding-tables TED Talks to traffic-jam-causing rallies with chanting and fireworks?

You see, Andrew Yang was not supposed to blow up.

With no money, name recognition, or experience, any political expert or casual observer would tell you he was *supposed* to perform about as well as the "Free Hugs Guy," who yes, also runs for president every cycle. When he announced his presidential run, Andrew Yang was variously laughed at or ignored, because he was *supposed* to be irrelevant with a field of twenty-nine elected officials competing in the Democratic primary. Even as he began to gain support, he was *supposed* to be a flash in the pan, at best, the male Marianne Williamson: a successful nonpolitician with an interesting story who showed up, got some click-bait press, and fizzled out.

Yet Andrew Yang didn't fizzle out. Not only was he not another Free Hugs Guy, he wasn't overshadowed by the seemingly endless list of established Democratic contenders.

Instead, our ragtag and inexperienced campaign team outlasted and outperformed four senators, four governors, seven members of Congress, two mayors, and one cabinet secretary.

And yes, I am well aware that Andrew Yang did not win the presidency. In fact, he didn't come close. He earned 5 percent of the popular vote in Iowa and dropped out after the New Hampshire primary. From a polling perspective, he was barely a blip on the radar—a small nuisance to more established contenders.

But Andrew Yang was more than just a presidential candidate, and the effects of his campaign extend far beyond any one election.

This book answers two related questions. First: How did Andrew Yang explode onto the scene in the first place? The answer to that is what fills in the gaps between our eighteen-person gathering in New York City in August 2018 and the seven-thousand-person rally in Los Angeles in September 2019.

Just as important, though, is a second question: How did a losing longshot candidate manage to stay relevant and influential *after* his longshot run? How is it that the majority of American voters are now in favor of universal basic income,[2] and Andrew Yang remains one of the best-liked and most influential politicians in the entire nation? Let me repeat that: someone who *no one had heard of* three years ago, who has yet to win a single election,* is one of the most popular politicians in the US—right behind former presidents Bill Clinton and George W. Bush.[3] More significantly, when the entire world was in crisis after the outbreak of COVID-19, we turned to the ideas that Andrew Yang's campaign helped mainstream. Instead of simply following the traditional playbook of government-aid programs or bailout money directed to businesses (see both the 1933 New Deal and the 2008 recession), the decision was made to give direct cash to citizens during one of our country's darkest hours. The idea was so popular that politicians and pundits on both sides of the aisle, heck even the pope himself, publicly announced their support of cash relief.[4] At the time of this writing, the United States government

---

* Oh yeah, we're going to talk about his mayoral bid too.

has already distributed stimulus checks of $600, $1,200, and $1,400 directly to millions of American adults, and is currently paying families $250 to $300 per month per child through the enhanced child tax credit, the closest thing to implementation of universal basic income we've ever seen.[5]

So how did Andrew Yang go from nobody to national, lose his primary bid, and end up more influential than some of those he lost to?

Was it pure luck? Good timing? Is he a mad genius? What?

The answer is none of the above.

We didn't overcome the massive odds stacked against the Yang campaign simply through a series of accidents. Sure, as with any success story, there's a decent amount of luck involved. After all, I was the youngest and most inexperienced major presidential campaign manager in US political history—I won't pretend that I always knew what I was doing. We made plenty of mistakes along the way, and I'll share these to hopefully spare others from making the same ones. But our campaign also made calculated strategic moves that set our candidate and message up for short- and long-term relevance. And we did that by recognizing that the game has changed. Politics does not work the way it once did. Traditional political gatekeepers are not as powerful as they once were. Marketing does not work the way it used to. Mainstream media is not as trusted as it once was. Frankly, many of the principles that were once the foundation of any serious political brand are crumbling. We were successful beyond anyone's wildest imagination by playing a different game entirely, one based on the knowledge that, in today's world, what matters above all is **building a brand that supporters identify with.**

Simply put—Andrew Yang didn't just run for president. Andrew Yang built a brand and a movement.

Our team evolved political campaigning for the twenty-first century— borrowing tactics from traditional methods that still work, and letting go of what didn't, in order to successfully turn a longer-than-longshot into a serious political contender. In the process, we created a playbook that can be used to help any longshot contend for anything. That's why this book is more than just a behind-the-scenes campaign story (for that, watch the documentary or listen to our podcast, *Forward*). The lessons we learned on this campaign are for anyone trying to build and sustain a brand, a business, or a mission. They are insights you can apply not only to attract new supporters, customers, or voters, but to keep them amid a flurry of distractions. This book will not only explain how Andrew Yang came out of nowhere to achieve national relevance, but also what we—as politicians, businesses, and people—can learn from his surprising breakout and sustained influence in one of the most competitive arenas in the world.

In other words, this book is a playbook for how to compete in today's "attention economy." And the best place to start, frankly, is there, with the attention economy itself—what it is, how it's changed our world, and how all this led me to make the ridiculous decision to quit a job I was good at to do something I knew literally nothing about: running a longshot presidential campaign.

Let's dive in, shall we?

1

ODDS ARE, NO ONE CARES
Welcome to the Attention Economy

Yang2020 job interview transcript, 2018:
Me: *Have you thought about how you think you could help
    the campaign?*
Potential hire Carly Reilly: *To be honest, I literally googled
    "what do people do on a presidential campaign?"
    before this interview.*
Me: *Yeah . . . You'll fit right in.*

MY JOURNEY AS A COMPLETELY INEXPERIENCED CAMPAIGN MANAGER FOR AN unknown candidate began, perhaps unsurprisingly, with a completely ridiculous idea. A ridiculous idea that nevertheless cut through every other thing that was laying claim to my attention, and got me to deeply, fundamentally care about it. This idea got me to care so much, in fact, that I quit my job to embark on an adventure that I'm not sure anyone could have been truly prepared for (and that I definitely wasn't).

Eventually, an understanding of how to capture attention this way would become part of our campaign's most powerful strategy, but our story truly begins in April 2017, at a small dinner in the private basement of a bougie restaurant in New York City's West Village, long before there was a campaign at all, and certainly before we'd figured any of this out.

I walked into said dinner after a long day of work as the head of client philanthropy solutions at UBS Wealth Management. Dressed in my typical Wall Street-asshole look—navy-blue, European-cut Suitsupply suit; evenly pressed, bright-blue Charles Tyrwhitt shirt; no tie; tan Allen Edmonds Strand cap-toe oxfords—I was a few months away from my thirtieth birthday, a little too confident in myself, and not nearly as much of a finance bro as I appeared.

The event was supposed to be a "Jeffersonian roundtable discussion," which is a pretentious way of saying "exclusive" and "focused on a specific topic." There were about fifteen attendees, all there to discuss "the future of work" . . . and then, Andrew Yang walked in.

When he did, I cursed under my breath. *DAMMIT! Not Yang!*

––––––––––

Let me backtrack. To understand why I had this reaction, you have to understand why I was at that event in the first place and how I got there.

Both my dad and my paternal grandfather were engineers, stemming from a long line of hardworking math and physics nerds who were good at problem-solving—and builders at their core. My mom was a special education teacher, a PTA supermom, and is the daughter of a cop and a nurse.

Mainly because of my parents' backgrounds, I grew up pretty interested in the intersection between society's economic and altruistic values—or frankly, how we balance what helps people and what makes money. I even majored in public policy, and when I graduated from college in 2010, I had exactly two job offers: I could work with special needs kids in post-Katrina New Orleans as part of Teach for America making $35,000 a year, or I could work on Wall Street at UBS Wealth Management for a cushy six-figure salary. I hated this choice—between actually helping people and not making any money, or making money and not really helping anyone. But, like most young Americans graduating from college, I had a mortgage's worth of student loans, so I regretfully decided that saving the world would have to wait, and I went off to sell my soul to the gods of capitalism on Mount Wall Street.

After I took the UBS job, I started volunteering a lot—I needed a way to make myself feel better about the fact that my job just made rich people richer. One of the places I volunteered was a middle school in Brooklyn near Coney Island. A few months in, we gave our students a survey, which included a question I had been asked myself as a child hundreds of times:

What do you want to be when you grow up?

I was expecting doctor, lawyer, teacher, astronaut—what I thought of as the usuals for middle school kids. But instead, the vast majority of answers were "professional athlete" or "pop star."

Now look. Who doesn't want to be Beyoncé? I get it. And I mean, I had just graduated from college, and I still didn't really know what I actually *wanted* to be. But these teenagers didn't even know what they *could* be. And as I got to know them, it became clear that they had no idea of how to get from where they were to any specific career—if "doctor," "lawyer," and "rapper" all seem equally far-fetched, why not aspire to be Nicki Minaj? And that broke my heart.

Let me be clear: This isn't some bullshit boo-hoo story about a rich white kid who finally saw poor kids for the first time and had his come-to-Jesus moment. I grew up in West Hartford, Connecticut—not in the wealthy part of the state near NYC—and spent the majority of my childhood in the working-class area outside of Hartford called Elmwood. I went to a public school where more than 30 percent of the student body was on free and reduced lunch and almost half of my classmates were people of color. When I competed around the state—in football, hockey, and baseball, along with nerdy stuff like jazz band, choir, musical theater, and a cappella (yeah, you can compete in those, too)—we all hated the rich kids, the kids with the brand-name equipment, the brand-new musical instruments, the fancy buses/arenas, etc., because most of us didn't have any of that.

Of course, I was well aware of how blessed I was: I may have had secondhand equipment, but I still had the ability to pursue all those extracurriculars in the first place. I had two amazing parents who loved me and a safe home to live in. I'm also white, male, and six foot four. This is the hand to be dealt in the United States of America.

But from my limited perspective as a kid, I felt like I had it kinda hard—I certainly didn't think of myself as someone who grew up with money. Money was the one thing my parents fought about. My dad scraped together almost every penny he had so I could play hockey, and I got teased for having used gear that was too big and out of style. I was a paperboy for the *Hartford Courant*, while also lifeguarding and working as a host at Chili's. My first car was a 1992 baby-blue Dodge Caravan that couldn't go faster than thirty-five miles per hour. I paid for most of my college tuition with student loans and scholarships. I interviewed for jobs with a fifty-dollar Jos. A. Bank suit that didn't fit and twenty-dollar loafers from JCPenney, and only got my interview with UBS because there was a glitch in the student registration portal that let me sneak into the last remaining spot. When I moved to New York City in 2010, I had nearly $200,000 in debt, $200 in my bank account, and lived off dollar-slice pizza and homemade crockpot chili for my first year. And for the record, I still believe Olive Garden is a nice restaurant.

I tell you this not because my background is particularly sympathetic or interesting, but because I do think it gives helpful context: while I knew I had it better than a lot of people, all those money issues meant I grew up with a pretty sizable chip on my shoulder, deserved or not. I worked as hard as I could, and eventually, I made it out of my hometown, went to college, and got a job in a big city to pay off my student loans. America's broken economy made things challenging enough from my starting point, so I honestly believed I had overcome a lot.

But working with these middle school kids was a punch in the gut. I didn't know poverty. I only knew the average American financial struggle, the one where things are rough, but there is an expectation that perseverance will pay off, and that there is reason to be hopeful about the future. Sadly, even this mindset is a luxury for many today. I was fortunate enough to be optimistic about my future, not to mention have an awareness of the path I might take to that future, one that includes more career options than athlete and pop star.

Meanwhile, UBS was basically printing money. In one quarter, my small team of twelve people earned over $250 million in fees, so I suggested to my manager that we do something like a team volunteer day to give back. He didn't seem to care, but said "sure" . . . then tasked me with finding something for us to do.

So I started looking into the options, and quickly realized how much companies suck at volunteering. We could arrange for employees to do things like pick up trash, serve soup, "help" build a house—one person suggested that we scrape barnacles off the side of the *Intrepid* (the military boat museum on the Hudson River). It is hard to get a big group of busy people to volunteer in the first place, and not only were these activities boring and labor-intensive, but it also it seemed like a poor use of time to have some finance bro spend an afternoon (poorly) framing a roof—why not leverage the skill sets that these employees actually had?

As this book goes on, you'll see examples of what I'm good at, and what I'm bad at.

I'm good with people, I've got lots of infectious energy, and I'm great at seeing the big picture. Understandably, I was great at group projects as a kid.

My weaknesses are mainly my strengths in excess: if something's too small to matter for my ten-thousand-foot-level brain, I struggle to give it the time or attention to detail it deserves. I can be careless with my words when I'm excited, and my extroversion can take over and make less outgoing people feel sidelined.

This situation played right into my strengths. I saw two problems—my kids in Coney Island could use some career awareness, and my colleagues at UBS (and corporate America in general) could use some better volunteer days.

So, while still working full-time at UBS, I cofounded a nonprofit organization with a teacher friend of mine. We called it SuitUp. Basically, we run one-day business competitions where kids solve a real problem for a real company—like creating a new shoe for Nike or marketing new headphones for Beats by Dre—with volunteers serving as coaches.* This became my passion project for years; I nearly left UBS to run it full time.

And that's how I first met Andrew Yang back in 2014. I needed board members to show that SuitUp was legit. My roommate at the time worked at Venture for America, so I got myself a meeting with Andrew and told him about SuitUp. That meeting was a perfect example of what I love about Andrew, the way he sees things clearly and takes action:

Andrew: "Your idea makes sense. I love it! How can I help?"

Me: "Do you mind joining our board? I could use your name to show we're legit."

Andrew: "Done!"

That simple.

Anyway, my boss at UBS eventually offered me a job helping run our client philanthropy advisory team—simply put, helping rich people give money to charity. I went to a lot of networking dinners looking for new things to present to our über-rich clients as a way to use their vast wealth for good. And over the years,

---

* Volunteers coach the students to create their business ideas and pitch them to judges. The winning team gets real money—it's like *Shark Tank* for kids. Since the companies (including Facebook, NBCUniversal, and Goldman Sachs) paid for the events, we're sustainable and growing, allowing us to give opportunities to more kids. We now have thousands of letters from students, teachers, and parents telling us how SuitUp helped kids focus their efforts toward a career they're passionate about. Plus, we partnered with a number of leading educational organizations already doing great work in these communities. Today I'm proud that SuitUp employs ten full-time staff, has impacted tens of thousands of students, and will be a million-dollar nonprofit organization by the end of this year (2022).

I had brought Andrew Yang to a number of client events to pitch his nonprofit, Venture for America.

Which catches us up to where we started, with me, a decade after college, dressed like a finance douchebag at a pretentious "Jeffersonian roundtable" dinner in Manhattan, cursing under my breath at the mere sight of Andrew Yang.

You see, by then, I had heard his Venture for America schtick so many times, I could probably recite it myself from memory:

> *Today, our top college graduates usually do the same six things in the same six places. Law, medicine, business school, banking, consulting, and Teach for America, and they do them in New York, San Francisco, Boston, Chicago, DC, and LA. We need to create a path for our top talent to create businesses in the cities hurting most now, like Detroit, Cleveland, Baltimore, New Orleans, and more, and give them the skills to start businesses in those locations.*

Honestly, it's a great pitch. Venture for America was training talented young graduates to create businesses in cities that desperately needed job creation. But I hadn't given up an evening just to hear that pitch again.

So when Andrew started to speak, I tuned out. *Yada yada yada, jobs, VFA, smart people build things, etc.*

But then he moved past Venture for America—and I found myself tuning back in.

"What are the most common jobs in the United States today?" he asked. Guests started guessing—*Fast food! Health care!*—but it is clear that we aren't quite hitting the answers. So Andrew guided us.

"Number five is manufacturing; number four is truck driving; number three, food services and food prep; number two is retail; and number one is administrative and clerical work, including call centers. What do these jobs have in common? They are all ripe to be automated, if they haven't been already. Half of American adults work in one of these five job categories."

Whoa. I was definitely listening now. He continued, checking them off on his fingers:

"Manufacturing is the one everyone knows about, where this has been happening for decades. Automation of manufacturing jobs has already devastated the economies of Michigan, Ohio, Wisconsin, Pennsylvania, and more—all states Trump needed to win and did win in 2016.

"Truck driving is the most common job in twenty-nine states; the vast majority are men without a college degree. My friends in Silicon Valley are working on trucks that can drive themselves.

"Food services will be one of the next to go—there are pizzerias that do not have a single person making the pizza.

"Retail is terrifying: we've all seen the self-checkout kiosks at CVS and our malls closing as shopping moves online. The average retail worker is a thirty-nine-year-old woman making about twelve dollars an hour. What is her next move when her store closes?

"And call centers are obvious—AI is getting closer and closer to replacing the average call-center worker, and it will be devastating for millions."

The more Andrew spoke, the more focused the room became. Anyone who has listened to him on a podcast or in an intimate setting knows this feeling. He had everyone's attention, even the waitstaff.

"The media has given us a number of reasons for Donald Trump's election in 2016, but I'm here to tell you a story that isn't being told. We've heard racism, xenophobia, Hillary Clinton, and anxiety about job loss to immigrants. But folks, the root cause is none of these things—it's robots. There is a direct correlation between the loss of manufacturing jobs due to automation and the movement to Trump. You see it in Michigan, Ohio, Pennsylvania, and Wisconsin—again, all states that went from blue to red in 2016.

"We are in the third inning of the greatest economic transformation in our nation's history—what experts are calling the fourth industrial revolution. It has already devastated our factories and led us to a Trump presidency. It is coming for our restaurants, our malls, and our economy at large. We must coordinate a nation-scale response before it is too late."

The room was in awe. We'd just heard Andrew Yang drop what I would come to call the "automation bomb." It's a story that, once you hear it, feels both startling and absolutely obvious. And given that Donald Trump had just become our president a few months prior, it was hitting a relatively fresh wound. It was like Andrew had parachuted in from outside the elitist bubble we were all occupying and explained what the hell was happening to our society.

No one really knew what to say, and before we could figure it out, he kept going.

"The third inning of this transformation brought us Trump. By inning five or six, you're looking at trucks driving themselves on the highways, which will mean millions out of work. We don't want to know what the late innings look like if we do nothing as these changes accelerate."

At this point you could hear a pin drop in between his sentences.

"The reality is this. We need to rewrite the rules of our economy to work for us, the people—not companies and their profit margins. We need to get resources into the hands of those whose livelihoods are at risk so they can adapt to this new landscape. And we need to do it all as soon as possible."

The room was totally on board. *Absolutely. Tell us how, Andrew!*

"Because of this, I'm running for president in 2020 on a platform of universal basic income."

And there it was. The completely ridiculous idea.

Of America? was my immediate thought.

It was absurd, of course. Running for president is an insanely difficult undertaking for even the most experienced and well-known politicians. Andrew wasn't experienced, well known, *or even a politician.*

The others in the room, predictably, had similar reactions, although everyone was relatively polite to Andrew's face. They spent the rest of the night trying (not always successfully) to mask their disbelief and dismissiveness while asking Andrew questions about automation, universal basic income, and how the hell he planned to run for president. Andrew answered them gracefully and logically, as usual. He talked about his upcoming book and said he planned to officially announce his candidacy in early 2018.

No one actually took him seriously that night, at least not as a presidential candidate . . .

Except for one idiot.

Yup, yours truly.

For some reason, what he said landed with me—hard.

Because I saw it. Clear as day.

Maybe it was because I grew up in a Republican-leaning household. Or because I knew plenty of friends from my hometown who felt frustrated and left behind by our changing economy. I remembered telling my entire team at UBS that Donald Trump had a real chance to win in 2016, and being laughed out of the room. My NYC team on Wall Street could not fathom a Donald Trump presidency, but I always thought it was possible. That night, Andrew's claims resonated with the part of me that knew the economy wasn't working. It had barely worked for me ("get a job on Wall Street" isn't exactly a widely applicable solution), and I'd had it easier than most people; I believed it shouldn't be that hard for anyone. I also believed that, if someone could just stand up and say it—intelligently, authentically, and while offering real solutions that could actually work—millions of Americans would know the truth when they heard it.

At the end of the dinner, I walked up to Andrew.

"I loved what you said. Have you built out your team yet? Can I get involved?"

———————

About a month later, on June 8, 2017, Andrew and I met at coffee shop in midtown Manhattan. The first thing he did once we were seated at our small table was slide me a copy of *Raising the Floor: How a Universal Basic Income Can Renew Our Economy and Rebuild the American Dream* by Andy Stern.

"Read that," he said. "You need to know all about universal basic income, how it works, and why it matters. This book sold me on it."

I'd come prepared, too—with a list of questions I'd assembled in the Notes app on my phone:

You're serious about this, right?
What's your plan? What's the end goal and how do you get there?
What about fundraising? I'm good with people but I don't have a personal network large enough to raise the millions needed—what are your expectations?
Do you have any skeletons in the closet I need to know about?

"Yes. I'm serious about this and I intend to contend," Andrew told me between bites of a brownie he'd bought at the counter. He proceeded to get brownie crumbs all over himself and the table (making a classic Andrew Yang snack mess of the sort I would eventually get used to cleaning up) as he broke down his plan to attack a presidential primary.

"Like everything else in this country, politics revolves around the almighty dollar. You raise enough money—you're a major presidential candidate. So all we need is a lane. We find our lane, we can raise money and contend at a high level.

"Now, what's our lane? To start, it'll be techies and Asian Americans. The tech community loves UBI, and Asian Americans will be excited about the first Asian Democratic candidate. They will be our fundraising base."

He started tapping his phone with brownie-crumbed thumbs.

"What do you think the 2020 Democratic primary is going to look like? It's going to look a lot like the Republican field in 2016. There will be twenty candidates, likely more. So with that in mind, take a look at the 2016 Republican field."

He flipped his phone around to show me an infographic from the *Washington Post* showing the 2016 Republican candidates and how much money each had raised.[1]

"There are very credible candidates here with fundraising numbers that we can match. If you eliminate super PACs, a lot of these candidates only raised a few million from actual people, didn't ever really poll above 5 percent, but were still considered serious contenders."

He wasn't wrong. A number of the major Republican candidates like Rick Santorum ($1.9 million), Mike Huckabee ($4.2 million), Lindsey Graham ($4.9 million), and Rick Perry ($1.3 million) hadn't raised much in individual donations. Even Carly Fiorina ($12.1 million) and Chris Christie ($8.6 million) hadn't lit the fundraising world on fire. Yet they were mainstream names who were taken seriously by the Republican party and the press.

"Democrats don't take super PAC money, so it will be a very similar picture for the fundraising landscape in 2020. If these numbers hold true, I believe that even if we raise just two million dollars, I can be serious enough to the press and develop a small base of support. If we do that, I can be a major candidate, hopefully make the debates, get the message out, and then, to be honest"—he put his phone away and ate the last bite of his brownie—"once I'm a serious candidate, the sky's the limit.

"I can raise two million dollars.* It will be a stretch, but I can find a way. And as for skeletons in my closet, I have none. I'm a boring guy. I don't drink. I don't

---

* I figured this is a good place to talk awkwardly about how rich Andrew is. Andrew is rich, but not "fund your own presidential campaign" rich. The press didn't help with this narrative, often referring to Andrew as a "billionaire" or a "successful tech entrepreneur." This drove me nuts, as it was at least lazy and possibly even racist to try to slot him into a stereotype of "crazy-rich Asian" or "Asian tech bro," since neither was true. Andrew created an education company that helped people prepare for business and law school, and he sold that to a public company for a few million dollars. So (a) it wasn't a tech start-up, and (b) he wasn't a billionaire. He is certainly richer than the vast majority of Americans, but not rich enough to pump millions into his own presidential campaign. Frankly, the only major thing he had in common with billionaire tech bros was a fondness for PowerPoint. Anyway, I digress.

smoke. I like basketball, hanging with my wife and kids, and I'm awkward and nerdy. I just want to help people—always have.

"Look," Andrew continued as he licked the brownie remnants off his fingertips, "I'm really excited about you coming on this journey with me. The world, and this country, needs entrepreneurs—builders and problem solvers—to get involved in politics. The politicians have no idea of what's about to hit us. And think about it—you've helped some of the wealthiest people in the world donate money in the hopes of making things better. Do you think philanthropy has any chance of fixing this problem?"

I didn't. For one thing, most people didn't know the fourth industrial revolution Andrew was talking about even existed. And I knew better than most what the limits of philanthropy were. This was a problem that could only be solved with government-level tools and scale.

"We can either go buy a bunker and hide," Yang said as he wiped his fingers on a crumpled napkin, "or fight like hell to put this fire out."

He put the napkin down and looked me right in the eyes.

"It won't be easy, but it's our only option. I'm going to send you my book when it's finished. Read my draft, read Andy Stern's book, think about it, and let me know if you're in."

We parted ways. I went back to my desk and couldn't focus on work.

While I could follow the logic, Andrew's plan was still fundamentally ridiculous. So ridiculous that . . . I couldn't stop thinking about it. Maybe it was because I was recently out of student-loan debt and looking for something out of the box as my next move. Maybe it was because I believed the world was burning and I didn't want to watch from the sidelines. Maybe I was just crazy.

Was I really going to help this dude run for president? Am I losing my mind?

Over the next few months, I kept in touch with Andrew and turned the question of whether to join his campaign over and over in my head, thinking long and hard and yet never coming to a decision.

Then, as promised, Andrew sent me a draft of his new book, *The War on Normal People: The Truth About America's Disappearing Jobs and Why Universal Basic Income Is Our Future.* I sent it to my brother, Jordan, to read at the same time—he's a year younger than me and my best friend. The plan was for us each to read the manuscript, draw our own conclusions, and then discuss our honest thoughts to help me make a final decision on whether to take the job. Very logical and regimented.

Until I launched myself out of my bed in the middle of reading it.

By this point, I was already sold on Andrew Yang as an operator and a fundraiser. I was sold on his mission in general, and on the concept of universal basic income. But all the concerns and questions that had been pulling at me as I tried to decide whether to make the leap from Wall Street to ridiculous—none of them seemed to matter after I read Andrew's book. The fourth industrial revolution was real. The problems Andrew warned of were coming and the world would have to confront them soon, whether Andrew ran or not. Maybe this campaign was a ridiculous idea, but Andrew Yang was right, and the sense of urgency I felt was enough to convince me to fight for it.

Jordan had a similar reaction. Or, more specifically: "If you don't take this job, I will never talk to you again. You can't talk about taking risks and fighting to save the world, look at this objectively, and not see it as the best possible option."

I called Andrew and told him.

"I'm in. Let's go save the world."

———

My first official day on the job as Andrew Yang's campaign manager was Monday, March 19, 2018, and I got out of bed with that *today is the first day of the rest of your life*–type energy.

I put on my fancy Wall Street suit, button-down, and leather shoes, and headed over to the address Andrew had given me—"My mom is in Taiwan and has offered us her apartment for a bit while we build the team and find our first office," he'd said.

I knocked on the apartment door.

No one answered. I knocked again, and heard shuffling. After a minute or two, a sleepy-eyed, half-awake Muhan answered the door in his pajamas.

"Oh wow, hey, Zach," he greeted me with surprise. "That's right, I heard you were starting today. Wow . . . you're early. Come on in, I still need to wake up."

Early!? It was 8:30 AM. I'd just spent eight years working in an office where you were in trouble if you weren't at your desk by 7 AM. Sometimes I'd had three meetings by this point in the morning! Muhan had now walked back upstairs to his bedroom and left me in the living room of the apartment.

If there were a physical embodiment of how low our chance of success was for this presidential campaign, it was this apartment. It was objectively too small for multiple people to work in while one of those people was also living there (namely Muhan, who had joined the campaign a couple of months before). It smelled like male body odor, soy sauce, and expired fish because someone—not naming names—had a thing for sushi for every meal. It was cluttered with stacks (and I mean STACKS—it was like a corn maze) of cardboard boxes filled with Andrew's just-published book. And seating options were limited to the previously mentioned cardboard boxes; a small, faded-blue love seat; a very uncomfortable wooden chair; and a tiny wooden rocking horse.

Looking back, it was a charming, humble beginning for our upstart campaign. At the time, my reaction was, *I left Wall Street for this? What have I done!?*

And that was how I started my experience on the Andrew Yang campaign: instantly regretting my decision.

After a few days of getting my feet under me, I finally thought I had a handle on the campaign organization, its finances, priorities, and strategic direction.

"All right, Muhan," I remember explaining to him while poring over a Google spreadsheet, "based on our current cash on hand and our burn rate, we have three months of operating runway if we raise zero dollars over the next few months. Six months if we continue at our same fundraising pace."

"Yeesh, that doesn't even get us to the end of the year," Muhan replied.

Then, right on cue, Andrew walked into the office.

"Great news, guys, we've hired Matt Shinners! He is one of the best LSAT teachers I've ever met. He's going to help us with admin and, more importantly, creating the greatest policy platform of any presidential candidate in history. Exciting stuff!"

Muhan and I stared at each other in shock.

I reluctantly adjusted the spreadsheet to include another salary on the books.

"All right, Muhan, based on our current cash on hand and our *new* burn rate, we have approximately *one* month of runway until we run out of money."

As stressful as this was, that's pretty much how Andrew built his initial team (I added "create a hiring process" to the to-do list immediately after this moment). The result was a group whose value-add was defined more by our commitment than by our actual experience or abilities.

Andrew had met Frawley—who moved from creative director, to digital director, to eventually building and managing our multimillion-dollar merchandise and branding operation—through a random connection in Manhattan.

He recruited Muhan—who started as our "tech guy," became treasurer, then chief technology officer, then head of human resources, and finally chief operating officer of a two-hundred-plus-person campaign organization—from Venture for America.

He met Matt Shinners through Manhattan Prep (his old company), and while yes, Matt was an amazing LSAT teacher, he also happened to be a supersmart policy wonk. He joined as our chief of staff, ran our communications team at one point, and eventually became our head of policy. He was further politically left than I was, balanced out my libertarian tendencies, paid attention to detail, and, as much as we absolutely couldn't afford him in the beginning, was worth every penny.

We all met Carly at one of our first campaign events. Opinionated, sharp, and intimidatingly well read, she kept us all on our toes; she started as our deputy chief of staff and in the early days filled a variety of roles managing advance, field, and volunteer operations. She was also one of the top cold-call fundraisers on behalf of her alma mater (Tufts University) in the school's history, and eventually became the finance director who helped us raise over $40 million in grassroots donations.

People have criticized the lack of diversity of our early staff. They're right: we were three white dudes, two Asian dudes, and one white woman—not exactly a great reflection of our society or the Democratic Party. But, to be clear, it's not like we had anyone else beating down the door to join this campaign. The six of us were very different people, at different points in our careers, connected by a passion for this cause. No one was doing this for prestige, or money, or even because they thought we had a realistic chance of winning the presidency. We all came to this campaign because we passionately believed in Andrew Yang and his message. Frankly, the main qualification to join our campaign team was that you *wanted* to join our campaign team—if you cared enough to be here, we hoped you could help us convince others to care about our fight as well.

Because unfortunately, we quickly came to a realization that would frame virtually all of our decision-making for the next two years of campaigning:

We are living in the attention economy . . . and in the attention economy, caring is rare.

That sounds dark. And I'm an optimist. But hear me out, and let me paint you a picture of our campaign in May 2018:

Andrew had just launched his campaign with a profile in the *New York Times*, complete with a photo shoot. His book, *The War on Normal People*, was getting rave reviews in various publications, as well as on Goodreads and Amazon. We went on MSNBC, Bloomberg, and Fox News—national mainstream cable outlets with millions of viewers. We had raised nearly $250,000 from Andrew's friends, colleagues, and immediate network, way more than expected for a crazy outsider running for president.

Yet none of these wins seemed to lead anywhere. We were raising less money by the day. We were laughed at, teased, and offered terrible unsolicited advice on how to do our jobs better from seemingly everyone we met. And worst of all, the vast majority of the time, we were ignored.

Our message was—is—powerful. We were talking about the end of our economy and society as we know it and why Trump got elected, and offering actual policy solutions to eliminate poverty and keep America from crumbling. It was an idea that the five of us plus Andrew were willing to drop everything and fight for . . . and still, no one cared.

The problem was that we weren't just competing against the other candidates (most of whom hadn't even declared at that point), we were competing against Netflix, Facebook, Twitter, TikTok, Kim Kardashian, the *Washington Post*, and literally any and every other thing on the planet that might attract attention.

This is the attention economy. And it is the world we all navigate and compete in every single day, whether we realize it or not. A world where human attention is a scarce and valuable resource. Where not only is our attention a finite commodity, but the fight for that attention is usually a losing battle.

Think about yourself—how often do you truly pay attention to something? And how much are you sifting through in order to do so?

When you wake up in the morning, you likely get hit with:

- Multiple text messages
- Emails—from work, from friends, from every online store you've ever visited
- News headlines on your phone or tablet
- Your calendar and schedule reminders

- Your spouse, children, significant other, or roommates asking you questions, telling you things, or adding to your to-do list
- App notifications on your phone, ranging from sports to weather to YouTube videos
- Local or national news if you turn on the TV or radio
- Countless updates on Facebook, Instagram, Twitter, or other social media apps you frequent
- Billboards, flyers, podcast/radio ads, and a slew of advertising in general during your commute

Before you even start your workday—maybe even before you have breakfast—your brain has filtered out hundreds, perhaps thousands, of stimuli. We are so used to it by now we barely notice, but it's an onslaught.

Never before in human history have human beings created so much content. According to *Fast Company*, in 2011, Americans took in the equivalent of 174 newspapers every day—five times as much information as they did in 1986.[2] And 2011 was a decade ago! With 90 percent of the world's data created in the past two years alone, demands on our attention are only increasing.[3] In contrast, the human brain still only has the ability to pay attention to a few things at a time. The University of Oregon did a study and determined that most human beings can only pay attention to four discrete thoughts at once.[4] Even the smartest among us can't keep up with the tidal wave of information vying for our attention every second.

And because we physically cannot pay attention to everything, we, as human beings with our own priorities, passions, and interests, simply tune out most of it.

It is only logical that more information and no increase in capacity to process it means that more things go unnoticed. But our economy requires people to notice things—you can't buy something you aren't aware of—so our entire world has now become a massive and accelerating competition for attention.

The sheer volume of demands on our attention has two major consequences:

1. The vast majority of the time, no one notices what you do.
2. Even if people do notice, it usually won't stick for long, because a new demand on their attention is always popping up.

Thus, to compete in the attention economy, you have two options for addressing these problems: **volume** and **relevance**.

We're all very used to **volume**—it's when we get beaten into submission, consciously or unconsciously, by someone or something trying to get our attention. We see this when Target emails us thirty times about the same sale. Or when the *New York Times* tweets about the same article a dozen times in a day. The hope is "if you didn't notice us the first time, maybe you'll notice us the second, third, or fifteenth." If we take more shots at getting your attention, we can score more goals. Everyone hates this, but sadly, it works. I'll touch on this later in this book when I talk about how Bud Light sells beer.

The second option relies on **relevance**, which is the means by which we all instinctively navigate the attention economy. In a sea of stimuli all asking for attention at the same time, relevance is the stuff that gets noticed because it's legitimately more interesting to us. "More interesting" doesn't mean better; sometimes it's something so ridiculous or terrible that you simply have to pay attention. *Can you believe he did that!?* Or, *Wow what a disaster!* TMZ and *Barstool Sports* are great at this. Sometimes it's simply something you find funny, like a clip from *Tiger King*, or it might be a headline about whatever crazy thing happened on your favorite show the night before, or a celebrity posting a video on Instagram.

Donald Trump is a perfect example of the attention economy at work, as he wielded both volume and relevance to get nearly everyone's eyeballs on him during his 2016 campaign. The volume of his coverage has been discussed ad nauseum, with cable news giving Trump a ton of "earned" media coverage that accelerated his path to the presidency.[5] The coverage was often negative, but it was consistent, keeping the spotlight on Trump and off his opponents—and in our attention economy, that was more valuable than less-consistent, positive coverage.

But the *reason* the press covered everything Trump did was relevance. Donald Trump wasn't just more interesting than Jeb Bush, he was more interesting than the new HBO series that had just premiered and whatever article was making the rounds on Twitter that morning.

In 2018, Andrew Yang was the complete opposite of Donald Trump, but not in a good way: almost no one covered *anything* he did, and when they did cover it, it didn't matter to anyone. Here we were, with this powerful message, a profile in the *New York Times*, a book that was selling well, and a handful of press hits on national news outlets to share our message on impending doom caused by automation. And literally no one gave a shit. We were dust in the wind. We sent email blasts nobody read. We hosted events that no one came to. We posted social media images that nobody liked.

Of course, we knew we'd be ignored by some people—what threw us for a loop is that even to the people who actually liked us, we barely registered. In other words, even most of our *supporters* didn't care—they may have agreed with us, and even wanted us to win, but not enough to do anything about it.

This was our crash course in the attention economy.

The question was not, "How do we stand out in a presidential primary?"

The question was, "How do we stand out in the *world*?"

This was not Andrew Yang versus Joe Biden, or Bernie Sanders, or Elizabeth Warren, or any candidate for that matter. This was Andrew Yang versus everything from Instagram influencers to *Hamilton* to Taylor Swift. This was Andrew Yang against a world where there is so much to pay attention to that people stop paying attention to almost everything.

Volume wasn't an option: we didn't have the reach or the money to plaster Andrew Yang everywhere.

Relevance was our only hope—but how do you make yourself relevant to millions of Americans in the twenty-first century when you are currently completely irrelevant by practically any metric?

Above, I said relevance is about "the stuff that gets noticed because it's legitimately more interesting to us." But the most important part of that isn't "more interesting," it's the last two words: "*to us*."

Sure, sometimes what rises above the noise to get noticed is more interesting just because it is funny or shocking. But most of the time, what we determine to be more interesting depends upon what we, personally, care about. And while something might catch our attention by being hilarious or novel, it's this other kind of relevance—personal relevance—that keeps our attention, and keeps it coming back. The catch is that as we start to pay more attention to things that are personally relevant, we also start to care less and less—about *everything else*.

If asked, most people could rattle off a long list of things they "care" about, but many of those will still lose out as they're pitted against each other in the attention economy. What wins, ultimately, is whatever is most a part of your identity. Think about it: Ask any ten Democrats whether they care about climate change, and they'll all say yes. They're not lying, but sadly, that level of caring isn't worth much in the attention economy. On the other hand, someone who sees the issue of climate change as a core part of who they are—they work at a climate change nonprofit, describe themselves as an "eco warrior," and/or wear slogan T-shirts about global warming—that person's level of attention to a climate change headline, advertisement, or call to action is going to be totally different than that of any of the ten random Democrats I mentioned before.

"To us" was the key. We believed we *could* get people to care about this campaign because *we* had all fallen in love with Andrew Yang and his vision ourselves. Somehow—despite the ridiculousness of his attempt to contend for the presidency with no money, political backers, or experience—we *identified* with Andrew Yang. We identified with his fight, his cause, his purpose. Because of that, we cared. We cared so much, we acted against our own professional and personal interests to drop everything and join this longshot campaign.

In the end, our task boiled down to this:

In a world where no one cares about anything, we had to get people to care deeply and personally about our candidate.

In the early days of the campaign, we began to see that in order to get other people to care about what we were building, we needed them to personally identify with it the way we did. In short, our group of political nobodies had to find a way to break through the all-encompassing and hypercompetitive attention economy to get millions of people to identify with another nobody—longshot presidential candidate Andrew Yang.

Simple enough, right?

I told you this story was ridiculous.

2

A CANDIDATE "LIKE US"
Introducing Identity Branding

Have you thought about running for local office instead of president?

—Practically everyone

It was May 2018, and Andrew was standing in front of a crowd of about twenty-five expensively dressed guests, clustered into the living room of a home in Santa Monica, California. It was the kind of house you see featured in pretentious *show-off-your-mansion* magazines, and it was filled with oddly shaped modern-art sculptures and furniture so fancy you're not supposed to use it.

This was the tenth fundraiser I had helped organize in the two months since I'd joined Andrew's campaign, and, just like the other nine, this one sucked. In fact, everything about asking rich people for money sucks. Allow me to elaborate.

The concept:
Here we were. Warriors for the people. Fighting for the millions of Americans who can't afford an unexpected $500 expense. Carrying the message that working men and women are being left behind by the changing economy, and advocating for our plan to fix it. And in order to do this, we had to stand in a multimillion-dollar home with an infinity pool eating expensive hors d'oeuvres (or whatever they call

the little hot dogs now) and begging for scraps from the 0.1 percent of American elites who buy furniture you can't freaking sit on.

The planning:

A common misconception about political fundraising is that you can just get a few über-rich people to write you six- or seven-figure checks. Not so—an individual's donations are capped (in 2018, the limit was $2,700), so this was not just about asking a few rich people for a lot of money, it was about asking *lots* of rich people for a little bit of money ($2,700 was a drop in the bucket for many of our event attendees). Thus, it started with us begging some wealthy friend, former colleague, or semi-acquaintance of Andrew's to host an event and pack it with other, ideally rich and politically open-minded guests. After a host committed, they would ignore my emails for a few weeks, I would hound them like a clingy ex-boyfriend, and finally we'd lock down a date for the fundraiser. Once that was settled, the host would begin *their* struggle to get anyone else to show up. Our presidential campaign basically started as an event-planning company, throwing events no one wanted to attend.

The questions:

The flow of these events was simple enough: people mingled, the host introduced Andrew, Andrew did Q&A, we begged people for money, people left. Sometimes Andrew took pictures with the attendees—not because they cared, but because we did. "Post this on social media!" we'd implore each guest, trying to sound light-hearted and encouraging instead of desperate.

The attendees were people who were *mildly* supportive of Andrew. Their attitudes ranged from, at best, *I love you, Andrew, and I'll do anything to help you (even though this is insane)*, to, *Aww isn't that cute, this guy's gonna try to run for president.* But even though Andrew and his ideas were received with mild positivity, the vast majority of our time at these events was spent being asked to justify the existence of our campaign:

> *Why should we donate to you if you have no chance of winning?*
> *We can't get anything done in Congress today, and you're an outsider with no connections there. How would you get any of this passed?*
> *Americans will never go for this. Isn't this socialism? Or communism?*
> *We already have an outsider businessman in the White House—why would we want another?*
> *How are you going to get your name out there?*

And, my personal favorite:

Have you thought about running for local office?

Don't get me wrong; many of these questions were fair. But it was frustrating to spend all our time answering them instead of talking about our message.

And then there were the *other* questions. The ones that felt like confirmation that these rooms were full of people who fundamentally didn't understand our message, our candidate, or even the state of the country. Questions like:

How are you going to explain this message to people in Iowa?

Seriously? The people in Iowa get this better than you do. They've been crying out for a change candidate—Obama, Bernie, Trump—for decades.

You're Asian. Won't people in Middle America dismiss you for your race?

This comment is deeply racist. Looking back after the campaign, we actually dealt with more racism in coastal-elite America (Democrats in particular) than any of the Middle America towns and cities we visited on the trail.

Now I know MY family would use this money responsibly, but OTHER PEOPLE may spend this money on things they don't really need, or even drugs and alcohol. How do you prevent that?

Again, there's a lot of entitlement baked into a comment like this. All data on universal basic income shows that people spend the money in overwhelmingly positive ways, but let's assume you haven't seen the data, AND that you're right—is it really your business how people spend their money? Besides, if you're out here plowing your paycheck into "don't sit on this" furniture, you're probably not the best person to be giving lectures on responsible spending.[1]

The advice:

Even worse than the questions was the unsolicited advice:

You need to get on TV more. Buy TV ads!
You should talk about why Trump is terrible more often.
You should talk more about abolishing ICE.
Have you thought about social media? You should get online more.
You need to go to college campuses. Like Bernie!

I got unsolicited political advice essentially everywhere I went, but these fundraisers were *the* most reliable spot to get "tips" on how to run the campaign—suggestions that were either bad, or that literally any campaign staffer would have already thought of—from people I had just met.

At one event, a donor pulled me aside and said, "Zach, I have a brilliant idea that I'm really surprised you're not doing. You need to make T-shirts . . . for college kids." That one eventually became a running joke in the office. Whenever someone was struggling with a problem, someone else would chime in with, "But, but, but . . . have you thought about T-shirts . . . for college kids?"

Now look, we had a no-name candidate, and I was completely new to this; we were desperate for ideas and always looking to get better, and I was definitely happy to get whatever help I could from people with more experience than me. But these weren't those people.

It blows my mind how arrogant most of us are when it comes to politics. Myself included. (Heck, I was so arrogant I left my job to run a presidential campaign, with no political experience whatsoever!) I get it—politics is personal to people. And not only does it affect us all, but it also doesn't *seem* that complicated. In areas like finance, medicine, and law, there's intimidating vocabulary, and understanding some of these fields at even a basic level can require years of schooling. But politics is a lot like sports: we're all active participants. *Sports teams need fans to support them! Politicians need us to vote for them! They use simple words and terms I understand!* We all have our political opinions, and we feel not only justified in sharing them, but qualified to offer them as advice.

These events felt like a weird alternate reality where the fans got to personally lecture the head coach. It was as if I could just walk up to Coach Sean McDermott and tell him which play to call in the middle of a Buffalo Bills game (something I literally want to do every Sunday in the fall).

But, like I said, I was new to the game and willing to learn, and we *were* asking these people to give us money. So I stood there and took it on the chin when some shithead millionaire in Gucci loafers, who'd read a *Politico* headline, gave me social media advice while he was three old-fashioneds deep after not donating a cent to the Yang campaign at a Yang campaign fundraiser.

And that wasn't even the worst part.

The end result:

Once we got past our initial roster of Andrew's BFFs—the people he was legitimately close to, who would support him regardless of how ridiculous the mission seemed—every single host had trouble actually raising money for the campaign. Lots of political fundraisers have an up-front charge for attendees—which we would have loved to do, but no one wanted to donate to the unknown Andrew Yang without meeting the guy in person. Many of our fundraiser hosts were as new to politics as we were, so they all started with grand dreams of selling $500-donation-per-person tickets, but in the end, no one was buying, so we let everyone in for free just so we didn't get embarrassed.

"They'll donate after they hear the message," the host would assure me. (They rarely did.)

"I'm not worried at all!" they'd proclaim. (They always were.)

But speaking to a room full of *potential* donors was better than not speaking to anyone at all, so we showed up, desperately, grateful to our hosts for trying.

The reward for our efforts? Our average event brought in a whopping $4,233—before expenses. Literally less than if the couple hosting had just given the $5,400 maximum donation ($2,700 each).

Through most of 2018, this was what running for president looked like for the Andrew Yang campaign. In a nutshell: traveling around the country to stand in fancy homes and beg for money from people who would ask why Andrew wasn't running for a smaller office instead, tell me I sucked at my job, and then donate nothing.

———

At the end of the day, being elected president of the United States comes down to a simple vote. But when you're *campaigning* for president, success is measured by polls, and polls are driven by three things: money, press, and crowds.

The best analogy I've heard to describe how this works involves imagining money, press, and crowds as three cars all connected by a strong chain. If one car, let's say money, is a superfast Maserati, it can pull along the other cars and help them pick up speed. That said, if the other two cars are 2000 Pontiac Azteks (this was the second car I owned—also a piece of shit) that can't get above third gear and break down every twenty miles, they'll slow the Maserati down. In other words, if you raise a ton of money but can't turn it into more press and bigger crowds, that will inhibit your ability to raise more money. But if you get a bunch of press, you can usually raise more money and likely start drawing bigger crowds. And when all three cars are moving at a healthy speed, you're really in business.

For most of 2018, an old Pontiac Aztek would have been an upgrade, as we were driving three 1992 Dodge Caravans, all of which struggled to move.

Crowd sizes were bleak. We could get about fifteen to twenty people to come to a public campaign "rally," many of whom we had to invite personally. No one knew who we were, thus no one came to our events.

Press was almost as bad. We'd had that *New York Times* article and a few other press hits, but Andrew remained virtually absent from 2020 election coverage.

The third car, money, was our best car and still pretty terrible. As of May 2018, Friends of Andrew Yang (our official committee to run for president) had raised less than $250,000, spent most of it, and had tapped out most of our immediate network for fundraising help. But while the fundraising numbers weren't good, money was theoretically the easiest car to move if we hustled hard enough. It was also existential. We had five full-time staff members on payroll and had recently started renting an office in Midtown Manhattan (one of my first moves as campaign manager was to get us out of the smelly apartment), so we were bleeding cash. Thus, we were resolved to the daily fundraising grind: call rich potential donors, ask for money, and get them to ask their friends to donate as well, whether through an event or otherwise. These rich potential donors who are the best at this are called "bundlers" and they run the money game in politics. Ideally you get bundlers to raise funds that you use to pay for travel, staff, and marketing, in the hopes of growing press mentions and crowd sizes. If you show growth, you can get more bundlers, raise more money, and so on. Again, this wasn't working for us in the slightest, but we did everything we could to stay positive.

And by "staying positive," I mean that Yang and I fed each other our own BS Kool-Aid to keep our spirits high while we traipsed across the country. In practice, it was me saying the following to Andrew after another fundraiser that didn't raise any money:

> *You really worked the room there. Those people warmed up to you by the end.*
> *One of the women who attended is the CEO of a really big company. I bet she's going to raise a ton of money for us.*
> *The photos from that event look awesome! I can't wait to post on social.*
> *The local reporter couldn't make the event, but she HAD heard of you! That's exciting!*

Or when I was down, it was Andrew saying:

The next fundraiser will be even better. I love our next host.
We're close to making the New York Times *best-seller list. That'll be huge.*
The Asian American donors—they'll come out for us. We can get them to donate
    in a big way.
Just wait until after the midterms, then people will give a shit.
Oooh look, [slightly well-known person] is following me on Twitter now. Our
    message is getting out there!

Yep. Glass half-full. Glass half-full.

I mean, hell. What else do you do when the world is laughing at you? Or worse, ignoring you? What are you supposed to say after you've flown six hours from New York City to Los Angeles with your six-foot-four-inch frame crammed into a middle seat in economy class because you're too broke to afford an upgrade, all for a fundraiser that didn't raise any money? You find whatever positives you can cling to, and you keep on trudging because you believe in the mission. At least, that was our strategy to cope with the fact that our campaign strategy wasn't working.

We were playing the same game that everyone else was playing—using the traditional model for running for president.

The problem was our candidate was anything but traditional, and this model was quickly breaking down.

In a sense, we were selling a new product to the wrong market. We were marketing the Andrew Yang campaign to the donor class. The political class. The people who thought Hillary Clinton was an appealing candidate for the entire country. The people who were surprised when Black Lives Matter, Occupy Wall Street, and the Bernie Sanders campaign became movements. These people didn't set the trends, they reacted to them (and many times profited off them). They were corporate American creatures of habit, and they would not get on board until the rest of the world told them it was okay.

They may have thought Andrew Yang had interesting ideas, but they also fundamentally believed that someone so inexperienced and out of the box could never have success in national politics. And, given that our country had *literally just elected* a reality TV star as president, it was clear that no amount of evidence would convince them otherwise.

This was the hardest pill for me to swallow. It didn't matter how good Andrew's stump speech was or what the campaign did—these people didn't care.

But as hard as it was to swallow, this was also part of the understanding that turned things around for the Andrew Yang campaign. It is what forced us to ask ourselves the question we raised in the previous chapter: If caring is rare in the attention economy, what can we do to generate it? How do we convince people to care?

And asking this is what led us to the realization we discussed in the prior chapter as well: that the key to competing in the attention economy is getting your audience to personally care about your brand by letting them *identify with* that brand—in this case, Andrew Yang and his outsider campaign.

We were knocking ourselves out at these events trying to explain to the wealthiest people in America that the country was in crisis. But these problems were so far away from home for them—they didn't need what we were offering, so nothing landed. Our campaign was about new ideas, a new perspective, and a new style of candidate, and no one in this market was identifying with that. The traditional political audience that every single candidate was vying for wanted nothing to do with us. So we needed to flip the model.

We needed to stop trying to convince a certain type of person that Andrew Yang was appealing. We needed to find and activate the certain types of people who Andrew Yang would appeal to.

We needed to focus on the people who would naturally *identify with* our campaign.

Once we understood this, nearly every single move we made was designed to allow supporters to identify, on a personal level, both with Andrew and his message. And we achieved this by deploying a concept I call "identity branding."

Most people, politicians, organizations, and, frankly, anyone or anything that needs to be branded, understand the importance of having a *brand identity*—a clear communication of what their brand stands for.

There are hundreds of books, websites, blog posts, and more dedicated to helping people build a brand identity. Any advertising agency in the world will tell you they're experts at doing this—determining everything from what text to put on a website or packaging to the colors, fonts, logo, and other visual elements that will best help customers understand what your brand stands for.

We already had a brand identity on the Andrew Yang campaign. It wasn't perfect (recall, Business Insider did call our logo "an abomination"), but it was clear enough: one look at our website or any campaign flyer and you could tell that Andrew Yang was an Asian man running for president who wanted to give every American adult $1,000 a month.

But to stand out in the attention economy, it's not enough have a solid brand identity. It's not even enough to have a brilliant brand identity with inspired ideas and fantastic colors and awesome services. If people do not feel a reason to connect with it, your brand *will* get lost in the 24-7 competition for attention. Today, your brand's identity is nowhere near as important as your supporters' ability to *identify with* your brand.

Identity branding is more than just having a strong traditional marketing identity. Simply put, identity branding consists of tactics and strategies that any product, person, or company can use to create deeper connections with their supporters and stand out in the attention economy. It is a specific type of brand identity that allows you to build an army of passionate supporters for your product (or organization, or candidate) and cut through the noise.

This concept, frankly, is the through line for the entire campaign. So let's break this down—what identity branding is, why it works, and how to do it—and most importantly, how Andrew Yang used it to go from anonymous also-ran to political superstar leading a national movement in less than a year.

Identity branding explained:
Identity branding is all about personal connection. At the risk of sounding cheesy—you become more than a brand. You become part of who the consumer is. People start to see themselves, or at least a part of themselves, in your brand.

My mom still calls herself a "Target girl." She loves shopping at Target enough to drive twenty minutes out of her way to go there instead of the Walmart down the street. She doesn't just do this when buying clothes or household decor items, either; she does it when buying paper towels, toothpaste, and so on. Why does she do this? Is it because their prices are better? No. Is their quality better? Not really.

My mom drives out of her way because she identifies with Target. Their brand is affordable and chic—you can look good without paying a fortune. Their target customers are women over thirty who, when complimented, will gladly tell you, "I got this at Target!" A person who shops at Target is stylish, but also smart enough not to pay an arm and a leg for a fleeting fashion trend. My mother sees herself as this person, and Target's commitment to affirming that identity for her helps solidify that connection. Target is not just a store my mom likes. It is a small part of who she is.

As another example, Apple has been leading the identity branding game for decades. We all know someone (maybe this is you) who will only buy an iPhone or a MacBook when purchasing a phone or a laptop. This is the definition of a sticky customer. It was an intentional strategy by Steve Jobs when he branded the company, and today the company's success is fueled by a passionate customer base that considers Apple part of their identity. Many of us remember the "I'm a Mac/I'm a PC" commercials. Mac was the cool, young, innovative, future-looking, awesome dude, and PC was the lame, old, behind-the-times nerdy guy. The commercial literally created an aspirational character that Apple's target customer could naturally identify with and pinned it up against its antithesis, who its target customer very much didn't want to be identified with. Now, after decades of identity branding, Apple can pretty much do what they want, and their customers will still buy their products: their headphones aren't great, they keep changing their chargers and forcing us to buy expensive new ones, they make it inconvenient or expensive to use Microsoft Office (the most popular software on the planet)—doesn't matter, they have a brand that people identify with.

But, Zach, there are plenty of successful brands that don't have "identity brands" yet make billions every year!

True. There are plenty of wildly profitable companies that have a simple brand identity that customers don't form a personal connection to. There are plenty of reasons to like a brand without identifying with it—simple reliability and familiarity, for instance. I don't think many people personally identify with General Electric, but they are one of the most iconic and profitable brands in the world. No one thinks of herself as a "Scotch tape girl," but lots of people reach for that brand over the cheaper generics.

However, in our case, we're not talking about established brands and organizations with existing customers who can trade on trust already built over time. We're talking about new brands trying to build an audience in today's attention economy—this can be a start-up, a new political candidate, or an established company looking to enter a new market and/or stay relevant. And in this new world, having an amazing new product isn't always enough. I can't tell you how many start-ups I've been pitched that have an inspiring entrepreneur, a great new prod-uct, and an untapped market for it, and still go belly-up. In today's attention econ-omy, having a great product is simply table stakes. Great products are irrelevant if no one cares about their existence.

Identity branding works because it allows you to generate relevance in the attention economy by creating a connection with your audience, essentially forc-ing them to care. When you identify with something, it becomes a small part of you . . . and instantly relevant, because what is more relevant to you than yourself? Nothing. Identity brands shift the focus from the brand to the consumer. Target's brand isn't just about Target, it's about my mom feeling thrifty and chic when she brags about her thirteen-dollar sandals that look cool at the neighborhood BBQ. Apple's brand isn't just about Apple, it's about the college kid posted up in the corner of the library and feeling cool because the logo on the back of his laptop is signaling to everyone around him that he's tech savvy and cutting edge. And when people feel your product is about them, they instinctively care, because everyone cares about themselves.

This pattern can grow upon itself over time. You identify with something, which therefore means you care about it, which therefore means it is relevant to you and you're paying attention to it, which increases your opportunities to iden-tify with it, and so on.

How to build an identity brand:
I'm not claiming to have invented identity branding. In fact, identity brands are not a particularly new concept—besides Target and Apple, you can easily look at Disney, Peloton, Air Jordan, and Tesla to see other examples. A number of the best brands in the world have grown by fostering die-hard fans who are extremely loyal, proudly support the brand publicly, and happily pay more for the product. Heck, even Nutella has people identifying with their brand, and they just made a tasty snack in 1964.

It's not new to politics either—Alexandria Ocasio-Cortez, Bernie Sanders, and Donald Trump have created strong identity brands. However, most often, this type of branding in politics comes as a result of success, not before it. Plenty of bands, musicians, celebrities, and athletes essentially have identity brands, but those brands often come in part from the fan base surrounding them, and politics follows the same pattern. What our team did differently was that we *intentionally* created an identity brand for Andrew Yang as a core strategy before we had any fan base at all. Doing this is what let us contend in arguably the most competitive arena in the world—American politics—and my hope is that anyone trying to compete in the attention economy can learn something from our efforts to apply this strategy.

There are three steps to intentionally building an identity brand. Each step is fairly simple by itself—it's putting them all together that's most challenging, and where the majority of our story takes place.

1. **Create a "like us" feeling—What is your brand's persona?**

    Most brands, of course, aren't people, which presents an extra layer of challenge in getting people to identify with them. Think about it: in a way, it is amazing that Apple and Target have gotten people to identify with a computer company and a big-box store, respectively. They do that by creating a clear persona for themselves—a set of qualities that they signal or represent, an overall character or "feel." These qualities are often aspirational: the things we identify with aren't necessarily a function of who we are so much as who we want to *feel* like we are—Apple may signal youth and cool, but you don't have to actually *be* either of these things to identify that way.

    So the first step in constructing an identity brand is to ask, *What is this brand about, and what feeling do I want it to create?* This sounds touchy-feely, and it is, but it's also effective. The simplest way to think about this is to imagine the phrase "like us" in front of the characteristics your brand represents/the feeling you're trying to create, instantly setting up the connection between your brand's persona and others who will identify with it. Some examples:

    - Apple—Like us, you are cool, young, design conscious, futuristic. Apple is about the cutting edge in design and tech.
    - Target—Like us, you are chic, smart, savvy. Target is about access to style.
    - Disney—Like us, you are whimsical, family oriented, hopeful. Disney is about creating a magical world.

    Notice that the feeling is not the same as the actual product. Creating an awesome product is one thing. Positioning it to evoke a feeling and identity is what creates an emotional connection, relevance, and sets you apart in the attention economy. However, one last point here—there is a difference between what you *want* someone to feel, and what they actually *can* feel from your product. Your identity brand has to plausibly reflect your identity. Disney's magical world of animation couldn't create an identity brand that reflected, "Like us, you're practical and realistic," for instance. The "like us" feeling must reflect what your brand can realistically do.

2. **Find your tribe—Focus on *who* wants to feel that way.**
The majority of business books will tell you that it's important to find the right target market. They're right. This takes that one step further, though. Effective identity brands don't just ask, *Who would like our product?* they ask, *Who would identify with our product?* In other words, who would want the feeling your product gives them? This is imperative because we're talking about identity—and it is what separates casual consumers from people who feel an emotional connection with your brand.

Certain people, no matter how hard you try, will not identify with certain things based on who they are. But this doesn't mean an identity brand can't appeal and expand to different markets. As a straight thirty-four-year-old male, I don't identify with Target, but I still shop there relatively often, and Andrew Yang eventually raised money from traditional political donors. But when we're talking about building your die-hard base of supporters, it's important to clearly pin down both what feeling you're evoking, and *who* could naturally identify with and respond to that.

Finding this tribe takes a good amount of creativity and work, as you'll see in the next chapter. Sometimes you'll have a similar tribe in a different industry that you can mirror—if you're Whole Foods, you may find future customers by targeting people who drive a Toyota Prius—and this is why Facebook's "look-alike audiences" have made them kings of advertising in the attention economy. Sometimes it might be a specific subset of an existing tribe—maybe not everyone who shops at Starbucks likes UGG boots, but teenage girls who drink Starbucks happen to be huge fans. Finding your tribe is all about knowing who wants the feeling you're evoking, then determining where and how to find them.

More often than not, and especially if you are trailblazing into a new market or offering an innovative product, your tribe does not fully exist yet. Andrew Yang brought a whole new group of people into politics who had never been interested before—there is not a single political analyst who predicted the market for his support. The reality is that people don't always know what they want until they see it. As the famous adage goes, "If Henry Ford had asked people what they wanted, they would have said 'faster horses.'" If traditional or existing markets aren't interested in your product, that doesn't mean your tribe doesn't exist. Great identity brands create their own tribes.

3. **Let them in—Invest in allowing your supporters to share that feeling.** This last step is the key, and it's the newest marketing battleground in the attention economy. Once you have a strong sense of your brand and the feeling you want to create, and you know exactly (or even generally) who identifies with it, you need to throw fuel on that fire. Successful identity brands will make significant efforts, invest substantial resources, and create useful platforms to let their new, passionate customers enter their world. The goal is to let your supporters become a part of your brand, give them a chance to meet others who feel the same connection, and empower them to share their experience more widely. As I loved to say on the campaign: *We need to take our supporters along for the ride.*

　　Frankly, there is no specific framework to execute here, as every product, market, industry, circumstance, etc., is unique. The ways to do this are infinite—from offering exciting customer experiences, to creating social media communities, to crowdsourcing ideas, and more—the tactics don't matter as long as they evoke the "like us" feeling you identified in step one, appeal to the tribe you identified in step two, and work in the direction of helping those supporters feel invited to identify with your brand. The bottom line is that you must invite your supporters in, and ideally inspire them to bring their friends. A simple example is Apple's new-product unveiling events. They're like rock concerts, and if you can't attend in person, millions of people watch them livestreamed online and then discuss on social media. I could give a hundred more examples, but I won't right now—you'll get plenty more through the rest of this book, because this is the fun part of identity branding. Regardless of how you do it, great identity brands intentionally create and foster a community around that identity.

So what did this all look like for Andrew Yang?

Well, step one—Create a "like us" feeling—was the easiest.

Andrew couldn't be all things to all people, especially in a crowded Democratic primary. Simply put, we needed to lean in to his unique strengths. What qualities did Andrew Yang stand for, and what feelings did his candidacy create for us to share in?

Visionary: Andrew saw the threat of the fourth industrial revolution, and our team felt like he was opening our eyes to major problems no one was talking about. *Like us, you're forward looking.*

Smart: Andrew was an unapologetic numbers wonk, and our team was intellectually curious. *Like us, you're fact driven and truth seeking.*

Nontraditional: Andrew was not a traditional politician, or a politician at all, and he valued innovation. For some people, this wouldn't have been a plus, but our team welcomed a break from the politics of the past and saw ourselves as future oriented. *Like us, you're not thrilled with politics as usual.*

Solutions focused: Andrew wasn't interested in rhetoric or winning political arguments, he was interested in concrete plans to help people now, starting with universal basic income. Our team was made up of people who valued entrepreneurial thinking and ideas that could actually work. *Like us, you care about solving problems, not winning political arguments.*

Optimistic: Despite the problems facing the country, Andrew was fundamentally hopeful about the future and the possibility of change—and so were we. *Like us, you're hopeful for a better future.*

This can all be distilled into something like what we saw for Apple, Target, and Disney, summing up the "like us" feeling or brand persona of the Andrew Yang campaign:

Like us, you are visionary, smart, nontraditional, solutions focused, and optimistic. The Andrew Yang campaign is about a new kind of candidate with out-of-the-box solutions that actually help real people.

Again, step one was the easy part for us. Andrew's identity resonated with everyone on our team and we were passionate about sharing it.

Our challenge was connecting step one to steps two and three, and our journey to intentionally craft Andrew Yang's identity brand faced its first challenges when we got to step two—finding our tribe. Because clearly, rich political donors—or even most traditional Democratic voters—weren't it.

We needed to introduce Andrew to a market, or tribe, who would naturally identify with him and respond to his message. And frankly, we weren't even sure if this market existed. At the moment, our tribe consisted of our tiny group of early supporters and inexperienced staffers—way too small to have an impact. Our tribe needed to start looking beyond the traditional political supporters and find some new recruits.

In other words—we needed to build an army.

3

TAKING SUPPORTERS ALONG FOR THE RIDE
Building the Yang Gang

Well, definitely don't call it "Yang Gang." I've worked in marketing for decades. And that's a terrible idea.
—Senior media executive

"WE'RE CALLING IT . . . 'YANG GANG.'"

Our five-person team was gathered in a standing circle in our high-ceilinged Midtown HQ in late September 2018, and I had just proudly announced the name of our new political army.

The responses were less than supportive.

"'Yang Gang' sounds like 'gang bang.'"

"Pretty sure most people don't wanna join a gang."

"This is the worst idea you've ever had."

I was undeterred. I raised my voice to be heard over their grumbling and continued. "When people voted for a Republican candidate in 2016, what did they say?"

Crickets.

"They said 'I'm voting for Ted Cruz,' 'I'm voting for John Kasich,'" I answered.

More crickets. I kept going.

"But what did they say when they were voting for the Donald? They didn't just say, 'I'm voting for Trump.' What'd they say?"

Blank, slightly skeptical looks all around.

Finally, Frawley came to my rescue.

"I'm MAGA," muttered Frawley.

"YES!" I jumped, excited that someone was at least pretending to follow along. "It was visceral. It was *part* of you. It is something you *identified* with."

"Yeah, but Yang Gang sounds stupid and childish and no one will like it," Carly piped.

"Can't we find something better?" asked Shinners as he rolled his eyes.

"I'm pretty sure Yang Gang is already a thing in Korea," said Frawley, looking at his phone.

No one on the staff was sold.

"Well, this is only a semi-democracy," I declared, indignant. "Yang Gang it is until you pick something better. You have one week. Otherwise . . . *Yang Gang*, baby!"

They didn't come up with anything better, because Yang Gang was brilliant. We needed to differentiate to create our identity brand, and Yang Gang was a creative way to give a unique identity to our supporters and welcome them into something that felt like a community.

I can call Yang Gang brilliant because it wasn't my idea. (I'm not always the best at generating ideas, but I am very good at seeing an idea's potential and putting it into practice.) The name actually came from Instagram—someone posted #YangGang in the comments on one of our posts, and I immediately loved it. So catchy. It rhymed, implied community, and invoked a sense of identity. It was perfect. Maybe it wasn't the best name for supporters of a serious presidential contender, per se, but it was perfect for us.

Regardless, we launched the Yang Gang name to our email list in the fall of 2018. This was how we began step two of creating our identity brand for Andrew Yang, by selecting a somewhat controversial* but catchy name that would help us,

---

* On one of our early trips to New Hampshire, shortly after we created the Yang Gang name in 2018, Andrew referred to our group of early supporters as the Yang Gang during a meeting with the editorial board of a prominent newspaper in the state. One of the most senior executives in the room chimed in immediately, "Well, definitely don't call it 'Yang Gang.' I've worked in marketing for decades. And that's a terrible idea."

and our new supporters, identify themselves as part of our tribe—a tribe that, unfortunately, didn't exist yet.

Now the question was . . . How do we actually build a Yang Gang?

At first, if I'm honest, we had no idea. We weren't entirely sure where to even look for our tribe. But we did know where *not* to look. We knew that we weren't likely to find potential Yang Gang members among the Gucci-loafer-wearing financiers and traditional political donors we had been trying to win over since I joined the campaign. Instead, the goal was to seek out those who would be more likely to identify with us—people working long hours at jobs that would never get them out of the massive debt they've accumulated for degrees they aren't using; people who understood the threat of automation; people who were ready for big, new ideas about how to make the economy work for everyone; heck, people who had tuned out of politics in general (or hated politics as usual). The goal was to find the people who would identify with our "like us" feeling, draw them in, make them feel like a part of something, and let them organize and build from there. It had to be 100 percent grassroots, passionate, different, and born from the same energy we all had when we joined this campaign: *This man is right. And I am going to fight to make his vision a reality.*

To find our tribe we needed to reach beyond the usual political audiences entirely, and that meant going beyond the usual places and the usual tactics.

And as a result, the Yang Gang was built through podcasts, memes, and math.

At the time, despite our best efforts to move the second car—press—from chapter two, cable news and mainstream media outlets were not having us on their networks. So we turned to a different marketplace for our ideas: **podcasts.**

The first large podcast we went on was hosted by Sam Harris, a neuroscientist, philosopher, author, apparently the world's most respected/popular atheist, and a podcast host with a cult following. Andrew joined *Making Sense* in June 2018, and he shared his message with Sam's more than two million listeners.

When the episode aired—an unedited hour-and-a-half-long conversation between Sam and Andrew, simply titled "#130—Universal basic income: A conversation with Andrew Yang"—we raised nearly $40,000 from over 1,500 people in just over a week after the episode. This was equivalent to more than 15 percent of the total amount we had raised over the entire campaign, and essentially ten times our average haul from a typical Andrew Yang fundraising event. Or, to put it another way, ten weeks of slogging from city to city for stuffy fundraisers had netted us a wealth of bad political advice from out-of-touch elites . . . and the same amount of money as a single ninety-minute podcast.

Podcasts were particularly well suited for Andrew because they let him get in depth about the future of work and society and explain his ideas fully. We weren't just fielding negatively phrased questions, or trying to condense the campaign's message into a sound bite. Podcasts are long form and intimate—you literally have someone's voice right in your ear! They offer room for discussion, and to listen, digest, and learn. I would argue there is no better way to get to really know what a candidate stands for, and no faster way to convert a low-information voter to a supporter/donor/volunteer.

Podcasts gave listeners the time and space to unpack and understand our message—and more importantly, become a fan of the messenger. In that way they were more valuable than national TV. Let me put it this way: by the end of the campaign, we had booked Andrew on every single major prime-time broadcast, cable news outlet, and late-night show in existence (except Jimmy Fallon . . . pretty sure he hates us), and, combined, we raised zero dollars and zero cents from all that time. At best, our appearances drove some mild traffic (one thousand to three thousand people per show) to our website.

Podcasts, on the other hand, were a fundraising gold mine. The day Andrew appeared on Sam Harris was, by far, the best single fundraising day of the campaign at the time. Then on February 12, 2019, he went on *The Joe Rogan Experience*, and, within one week, we had raised $250,000—almost as much as we had raised since the campaign started. Joe Rogan's podcast is so powerful you can argue it truly launched an entire national movement around universal basic income, channeled through Andrew Yang. By the end of that February, nearly two million people had viewed Joe and Andrew's two-hour conversation on YouTube alone—the audio version of the episode had been listened to by over ten million.[1] For an upstart campaign trying to find its tribe outside of the normal political world, you could not have asked for a better outlet. One month after the episode aired, we had raised nearly a million dollars, with an average contribution of $13.14.[2]

Reread that. Those numbers are absurd.

Yang hit most of the big podcasts in a few short months in early 2019—*The Breakfast Club, Freakonomics, Ben Shapiro, Pod Save America, H3*—many times speaking to audiences larger than the average nightly viewers of prime-time cable TV stars Rachel Maddow (MSNBC), Tucker Carlson (Fox News), and Chris

Cuomo (CNN) combined. Each came with an influx of new money, email sign-ups, and social media followers—growing the Yang Gang every step of the way. But as awesome as they were for us, podcasts came with their own set of challenges.

Podcasts were long. They were a commitment. Getting every voter we wanted to reach to listen to an entire podcast was unrealistic (especially since the message of job loss, automation, and a government that's not doing anything to save us isn't exactly uplifting), no matter how big an audience any specific podcast has. And usually, people listen to podcasts in private. They might discuss them a bit, on Twitter or elsewhere, but they're not inherently shareable, meaning our message wasn't growing much beyond the audience of the podcast itself. And, to be frank, as nuanced and deep as they allowed Andrew to get, they didn't add much in terms of political legitimacy. For instance, our Joe Rogan episode was sandwiched in between one with Colin O'Brady, a guy who solo trekked across Antarctica (cool, but odd), and an episode where Joe debated the benefits of medical marijuana with Alex Berenson (an author of several thriller novels) and Dr. Michael Hart (founder of a medical cannabis clinic in Canada). This was not exactly where you go to find the next president of the United States.

Thankfully, we were also able to grow our tribe through a very different strategy: **memes.**

Memes were the polar opposite of podcasts. They were short, fun, super shareable, and oddly very legitimizing (ask any famous person: you haven't truly made it until you're a meme). They fit our unique identity like podcasts, despite being totally different from them in almost every way.

Memes were not new to politics (Trump supporters made millions of memes in the 2016 election, largely to make fun of Hillary Clinton), but the *intentionality* of our campaign's use of memes was something different.

In 2020, Mike Bloomberg's campaign would spend a ton of money on making memes and buying placement on popular social media accounts, and many in the press praised it as a genius idea. But nearly a year before that, in early 2019, our campaign had already decided to make memes a core piece of our strategy—at one point we seriously considered spending a quarter of a million dollars to have Fuck-Jerry Media, one of the original kings of meme making, promote our candidate as a meme online. In the end, we decided it would be more effective and in line with our identity brand to make our own memes and empower our supporters to create them (we weren't rolling in cash either).

The key to our meme-making strategy was to use the fun of memes to actually communicate our policy message. Memes may not have been the best venue for getting in depth about Andrew's ideas, but they were perfect for disseminating our $1,000 a month/UBI core message. We needed our message to be shared far and wide—and fun memes about Andrew Yang and his free-money plan (which balanced out the doom and gloom of all the talk of automation) were a perfect way to spread a policy message on channels that didn't normally get political content. For example, if you visit a sci-fi message board, political posts are generally frowned upon. But if you post a fun Andrew Yang/free-money *Star Trek* meme on that board, chances are you'll get some positive responses, and maybe start a conversation in a group that doesn't usually talk politics or policy.

Now the important question: *How do you intentionally make your candidate a meme?*

As I mentioned, we initially thought we would have to do something like Netflix did with *Bird Box,* and pay social media accounts to post memes that we provided (hence the potential collab with FuckJerry Media). We tried creating our own Yang memes and posting them to some decently popular meme accounts, but nothing really stuck. We also tried creating our own memes and just posting them to our campaign social media accounts, but that didn't seem to go anywhere either.

But even though the memes we created didn't catch (likely because a meme doesn't feel as authentic when it's created by the official meme subject), what they did do was open the floodgates for our small group of existing supporters to start making memes of their own. Naturally, we leaned in to this by sharing these memes far and wide.

Because the real answer to getting your candidate to be a meme is stupidly simple: Let your candidate be meme-able.

I'll never forget the first truly awesome Andrew Yang meme we found online. It was a GIF posted by the Twitter account @RockToaster, showing the *Terminator,* Arnold Schwarzenegger (labeled "Andrew Yang"), riding a motorcycle on the highway, saving John Connor (labeled "US workers"), who's on a different

---

* Remember? That Sandra Bullock movie? It was one of the most discussed topics in the world for about a week, and now this is likely the first time you've thought about it in years. The attention economy, baby: we might become briefly obsessed with something that rises above the noise and then forget it like it never happened.

motorcycle, from a massive truck (labeled "automation"). Schwarzenegger/Yang pulls up full speed in front of the truck/automation, grabs John Connor/US workers with one arm, and saves the day—right before the truck runs over the now-empty bike and destroys it.[3]

It's hilarious. And it loops over and over.

We reposted it on all of our official campaign social media accounts—#YangGang, of course. And that's how we discovered we could use memes to find and grow our tribe.

"YANG CAN MEME!" I remember reading in the comments. Supporters created more and more memes, using the #YangGang hashtag, and we reposted the good ones. People tagged their friends, shared on their own channels, and our social media following grew and grew—as did the number of Andrew Yang diehards. This wasn't just growth, it was the right kind of growth, and the Yang Gang took off by making newcomers instantly feel like they were part of something. It was identity branding at work. Would you rather have one million people who vaguely know who you are, or one hundred thousand people who feel genuinely connected to you? Early on in a presidential primary, and in most business ventures, I'd take the latter all day.

So we were starting to build our tribe—we had depth from podcasts, and we had fun from memes. You couldn't write Yang off as a joke because we could talk in serious detail about the issues and our plans, but you couldn't dismiss him as "just another boring politician" either. We'd leaned in to our candidate's unique identity to reach and connect with our supporters, and it was starting to pay off.

But we were still missing something.

We needed to translate the fun and powerful energy we were building on the internet into an in-person political reality.

And this brings me to the last piece of the Yang Gang puzzle.

Math.

At the time, if you went to an Andrew Yang "rally," you essentially went to a TED Talk with a political banner behind the speaker. Yang was wonky. The crowd was too. Generally speaking, people would come, listen quietly, laugh a little bit, and applaud at the end.

And that was frankly to be expected when your candidate was saying things like:

"Well, I've looked at the numbers. Do you want to guess the effectiveness rate of government-funded retraining programs?"

And:

"We are going through the greatest economic and technological transformation in human history. What experts are calling the fourth industrial revolution."

Or the always thrilling:

"The average retail worker is a thirty-nine-year-old woman making between eleven and twelve dollars per hour. What is she going to do when her job is automated by robot kiosks?"

Seriously, reread those. How the hell do you get someone to cheer after any of those lines?

So the challenge was this: How do we go from academic TED Talk to energizing political rally speech?

Our first move was to try to get Andrew to stop talking like a professor and start talking like a politician. This was a bust out of the gate. We would write him full speeches, and he would read them, politely thank us, and then completely ignore everything we wrote. If we were lucky, 5 percent of our ideas might find their way into what he actually said at the next event. Yang loved to wing it, and scripting him was a waste of time—as our future political director, who was from West Virginia, would later say, "You can't make a dog quack like a duck."

Plan B involved just getting him to insert some exciting moments or one-liners into whatever he was already going to say. Things like:

"I am here today to bring that wave crashing down on Washington, DC's head. You are that wave. Will you create this wave with me!?"

Or even just:

"WHO'S WITH ME!?"

This also failed.

Imagine watching a TED Talk where the speaker is in the middle of an important, fascinating point on economic inequality, and then all of a sudden they start screaming, "WILL YOU JOIN THIS FIGHT WITH ME!?"

Whatever you're imagining right now, the in-person reality was likely even more cringeworthy. (I pray that you don't put this book down and Google Andrew Yang 2018 rally speeches.) The "excitement" felt so forced—actually, "inserted" is the better word. Like we'd cut and pasted it in, because we essentially had.

There's a difference between being a natural politician and a good public speaker. Andrew could be a brilliant public speaker, but "firing up" a crowd was a totally different skill set, and not one he had at the time.

What made this so frustrating was that, by early 2019, our newfound tribe *was* fired up. Think about it. If you went out of your way to track down Andrew Yang after listening to him on a podcast or seeing a meme shared on Instagram, and showed up to an event to find yourself surrounded by hundreds of other people who were also inspired by his vision, how excited would you be? The energy in the audience was always like, *Oh crap, this guy is for real! F yes!*

But because Yang was not a natural "ignite the crowd" guy, our team struggled to capitalize on that excitement. Our newly formed Yang Gang needed permission to get excited. Many Yang Gang members learned about Yang alone at first—shared via the internet in the privacy of their own homes. They needed to know that this wasn't just a random guy talking numbers on podcasts, or a fun meme about free money—this was the beginning of something bigger, and it was our job to evoke that emotion in real life. The last thing we wanted was for people to get excited about Andrew's message, come to an event, and leave disappointed.

The glue that brought the Yang Gang together came from the most random of places.

"What about 'math' signs?" Frawley piped up to the other four of us in the office one Tuesday afternoon.

Silence. No one had said anything to prompt that question. No one even knew what he was referring to. We collectively responded, *You wanna do what now?* without actually saying anything.

He said it again.

"We could make 'math' signs . . . for the upcoming rally. In Baltimore."

Instantly, it clicked. A vision appeared in my head of Yang spitting out facts and figures in his stump speech and people holding up these signs and yelling "MAAAAAAATH" while he did so. It *fit*. It fit because it wasn't about fitting in or turning Andrew into a politician, it was about being unapologetic about who we were and what we believed in. It was a perfect encapsulation of so many parts of our campaign's identity—it felt just outrageous enough to work.

So at the next campaign event in Baltimore, held shortly after the Joe Rogan podcast aired in February 2019, we created a bunch of different campaign signs in our signature dark blue, and laid them out for people to choose from when they walked in.

Here were the options:

ANDREW YANG for PRESIDENT

YANG GANG
HUMANITY FIRST

And of course:

MATH

Guess which one ran out immediately?

In the middle of his speech that night, Yang calmly launched into one of his usual lines: "And I looked at the numbers," he said . . . and the crowd started *screaming*.

"MATH!!!!!!!!!!" they shouted, waving the signs in the air and laughing. They *loved it.*

The best part was Andrew's reaction—because the thing is, our inexperienced team had forgotten to give him a heads-up on the whole "math" thing. So, taken aback by the crowd's ecstatic reaction to a line that had literally never gotten *any* reaction before, the usually unflappable Andrew Yang stopped midsentence. The cheers got louder.

"Yeah!" he yelled back, awkwardly.

More cheers.

Now, gaining confidence:

"All right! Let's do some fucking MATH!"

The crowd erupted.

And just like that, we'd solved our excitement problem.

"Because the opposite of Donald Trump," Andrew started yelling at the end of every speech, "is an Asian man who likes MATH!"

That's right. We found a way to get people excited about, of all things, fucking *math.*

And just like that, we'd found our tribe. Podcasts brought us a large audience of intellectually curious supporters. Memes shared our core policy proposals and authentically different candidate across the internet. And MATH helped solidify our new community's identity and create real-life excitement that brought supporters together outside of their computer screens. We were finally reaching people who naturally identified with Andrew and his message. Step two was complete.

From here, and for the vast majority of our campaign's story, our focus was on step three—doing everything possible to let our newfound supporters in, creating a community that would reinforce our identity and grow on its own.

Again, there is no perfect recipe here, but to start, we focused on what we were already good at: a strong core message with a unique messenger and a grassroots base. We poured our energy and resources into making it easier for the Yang Gang to identify personally both with Andrew and with a core message about the need for UBI. No one was going to authentically identify with Andrew Yang because of his stances on gun violence, health care, or foreign policy. We either didn't have the experience, there was no way to differentiate ourselves from other candidates, or other candidates had already made it their issue (i.e., Bernie Sanders and Medicare for All). Andrew's out-of-the-box message helped him stand out and gave folks another reason to identify with our tribe.

As we leaned on our message, leaned in to our unique identity, and let supporters in, we watched the newly formed Yang Gang respond accordingly. In practice, this is how it played out:

We leaned on our message of universal basic income—$1,000 a month for every American adult.

We put our money where our mouth was, and gave three families (one in each early primary state of Iowa, New Hampshire, and South Carolina) $1,000 a month for an entire year. In addition, we shared as many good $1,000/month memes as we could find. And most importantly, we made sure every single press hit was focused on Andrew's core $1,000/month idea—which we called the "freedom dividend" (Andrew found that the idea "tested better with the word 'freedom' in it")—to make sure the message never got lost. For all intents and purposes, Andrew Yang was universal basic income, and universal basic income was Andrew Yang. This made Andrew not just a candidate, but an idea.

Yang Gang response: Our tribe was made up of people who felt a sense of urgency around our message, and their passion for Andrew's ideas helped them overlook some of his weaknesses as a candidate (lack of political experience being the biggest). A vote for Andrew was a vote for money in your pocket . . . no, everyone's pocket! Supporters made massive cardboard one-thousand-dollar bills with Andrew's face on them, adopted phrases like "Secure the Bag" to reference Andrew's focus on universal basic income, and constantly created memes to share our core policy position.

We leaned in to the unique identity of our smart, nontraditional candidate.
We embraced our nerdiness, created MATH merch, and built an unmatched policy platform with more than one hundred policies, each simply explained on our website. Andrew was the anti-politician. He never wore a tie. He cursed. He welcomed supporters from all political parties, and we made T-shirts that said, "Not left or right, FORWARD." We let our campaign be fun.

Yang Gang response: Our core supporters loved talking about our ideas, and the Yang Gang used their strong social media presence to spread them. They weren't all college educated, but they had a desire to learn and weren't fazed by facts, statistics, and numbers. When someone online said something about Andrew that wasn't correct, the Yang Gang could reply with a link to his actual policy position on our website.

The vast majority had never voted for, volunteered on, or attended anything politically related. They didn't just come to rallies to stand quietly and listen to a candidate, they came to go NUTS for Andrew Yang. Over time, Yang supporters made crazy merch and signs and all forms of art. My favorite: some supporters had watched so many Yang YouTube videos that they noticed he made a "claw" with his hand when he talked about Amazon sucking up all the retail jobs . . . so they proceeded to make massive posters of "Yang Claws" and screamed "THE CLAWWWW" whenever he used it.

We let our supporters in and made them a part of who we were.
When the Yang Gang turned MATH into an acronym—Make America Think Harder—Andrew adopted it on the trail. We created blue MATH hats, then MATH T-shirts, notepads, mugs, and more. We created Facebook groups (Yang2020Basecamp) and Reddit threads (r/YangForPresidentHQ) to foster a sense of community among the Yang Gang, and we empowered volunteer moderators and Yang Gang regional leaders to promote and facilitate our events, messaging, and fundraising efforts nationwide. We did hours of live Q&A sessions, giving the Yang Gang intimate access to Andrew. He responded to comments on Twitter, called small donors personally, and would spend hours taking photos with every single person who came to a rally and

wanted one. We emphasized the need for our shared humanity to save us from the coming robot apocalypse, coining our slogan: "Humanity First." If this was a people-centered campaign, it needed to be people powered, and it was.

Yang Gang response: Our supporters felt a personal connection to Andrew, his message, and the campaign itself. They felt like a part of the campaign, like its mission was their own, and they shared in its successes (and failures) accordingly. And hell, who am I to say they weren't part of the campaign? We were reposting their memes and videos all the time—they might as well have been our comms team. I remember scouring the r/YangForPresidentHQ subreddit channel for new marketing strategies (most were kinda terrible, sorry Yang Gang), and even trying to crowdsource tactics. They coined the term "Yanged" for when they convinced someone to support Andrew. ("I just Yanged my Uber driver!") Eventually they started using a blue hat emoji on Twitter to signal to the world that they were Yang Gang, and would photoshop MATH hats on images of popular figures and celebrities who they thought were aligned with Andrew. They shared their designs with everyone and anyone who would listen, and we promoted their "unofficial" content on our official channels.

This is what happens when you create a strong identity brand. Supporters become deeply invested, and because there isn't such a hard line between candidate/voter or business/customer, it will grow organically on its own as supporters who identify with you engage and start adding their own personalities and ideas. We saw the Yang Gang create music videos, dances, street art, cryptocurrencies, Reddit threads, cartoons, YouTube channels, and more—you name it, they did it. The brand was built for others to identify with, and they *absolutely* did.

And, best of all, as alluded to earlier, their support was deep. Because the Yang Gang identified so strongly with Andrew Yang, they weren't about to shift with the political winds to support some new "flavor of the day" candidate. Whether they found us through a podcast, a meme, or something else entirely, all members of the Yang Gang got involved for the same reason—not because they were devoted to politics in general, but because they identified with Andrew and his ideas. In fact, one poll even found that over 40 percent of them had not planned to vote at all if it weren't for Andrew Yang.[4]

Our three cars were finally rolling. We got our own press through podcasts, sharing our message in long form. We built a following that helped us draw bigger and bigger crowds. And the money started flowing in. By the end of the first quarter of 2019, we had raised $1.7 million from eighty thousand donors—99.6 percent of those donations were less than $200, with an average donation of $17.92.[5]

Eighty thousand people. It had only been six months since that eighteen-person event in our new HQ. Now we didn't have a campaign wall big enough for the signatures of all of our supporters.

We'd built our identity brand—we created a feeling, found our tribe to share it with, and let them in to accelerate our growth. We had built an army. *Our* army. Andrew was no longer just a political candidate; he was a physical representation of a community who deeply identified with his vision and mission. The Yang Gang cared about the campaign and was paying close attention to everything we were doing; the Andrew Yang campaign had generated its own relevance.

And while we didn't know it at the time, this was only the beginning. We were on the cusp of building a movement that would take the entire political world by surprise for one main reason: we were playing a different game.

4

THE GAME HAS CHANGED
What Matters Is What Works

The main thing is to keep the main thing the main thing.
—Stephen Covey (and Zach Graumann)[1]

BACK IN OCTOBER 2018, A SENIOR *POLITICO* REPORTER COVERING THE 2020 ELEC-
tion wrote a piece on former HUD secretary Julián Castro, who was exploring a
presidential run. The article contained the following quote:

*Currently, only Rep. John Delaney has officially announced that he is run-
ning for president.*[2]

Which, of course, was inaccurate. We had declared our candidacy in February
2018—eight months earlier.

I wrote the reporter an email:

*Great article on Julián Castro this morning! Always great to read about the
competition.*

*Since you're covering the 2020 election, I wanted to reach out to intro-
duce myself. I'm Zach Graumann, Andrew Yang's campaign manager. I see
that you wrote for the* Daily Iowan*—we've had some great coverage there!
If you're interested in talking with Andrew about his campaign, or learning*

more about our platform, feel free to reach out to me or Matt Shinners, our
press director.
See you on the campaign trail,
Zach Graumann

This email embodies something we'd been struggling with since the beginning of the race. The question wasn't just "How do you *win* the presidency of the United States?" Nor was it even "How do you *contend* for the presidency of the United States?"

No, no, our quandary was an even more basic one: "How do you *become a candidate* for the presidency of the United States?" Because, apparently, filing the paperwork and getting an article in the *New York Times* was not enough to get included in *Politico* election coverage.

Sadly, writing emails like the one above, reminding people we existed, was something we did at least weekly, and Matt and I had the response process down to a science. This was a humbling experience because, by the twentieth email, there was no way to ignore the obvious conclusion: to the press, there was no difference between Andrew Yang and the Free Hugs Guy (Kenneth E. Nwadike Jr., who runs for president every cycle, as mentioned in the introduction), or Vermin Supreme (whose signature look was wearing a boot on his head), or Lisa Simpson (who'd legally changed her name to brand herself and her campaign like the *Simpsons* character), or any of the other "noncandidate" candidates. In fact, in the 2020 election, 1,212 people filed to run for president.[3] Of course, most voters only ever heard about a small subset of these candidates—those considered "serious candidates." This didn't always mean they had a serious chance of winning.

What they had (and what we desperately needed) can be summarized in one word: *legitimacy*.

A few more painful examples of how unserious our campaign was considered to be over the year following our launch in February 2018:

- **FiveThirtyEight:** Starting in January 2019, this popular political forecasting website ran a profile piece on each "major" presidential candidate (including many people we eventually beat). We were not included in the early rounds of these—despite our numerous emails to every reporter on staff.

- **Cable news graphics:** When discussing the election, cable news outlets displayed a large grid of candidate headshots to show who had declared a run (or was likely to run) for president. We didn't make the grid, even though a number of candidates included were polling at 0–1 percent (like we were), and even when the list included relatively unknown outsiders (like Tom Steyer) or elected officials with a very small following (like Eric Swalwell).
- **Polls:** We weren't even listed in early polls. This was the same "chicken-or-the-egg" problem we kept running into. It seemed like the way to be considered a legitimate candidate was to be treated like one (for instance included in polls) . . . which only happened if you were already considered legitimate. Polls were especially important to us, for reasons I'll get into shortly. We emailed pollsters daily, pointing that out. No luck.
- **Wikipedia:** Even the "2020 Presidential Election homepage" refused to acknowledge us! We would edit the page to add Andrew Yang's name, and a moderator would inevitably find it, delete it, and kick us off. It was embarrassing.

To be fair, legitimacy is an issue that all longshots deal with. You're fighting against people's expectations for you as a newcomer in any industry or endeavor. It's just that in politics, building our initial tribe through our identity brand wasn't enough. We weren't *just* trying to create die-hard fans; we needed those fans to propel us into becoming a legitimate option for them and many others to vote for. Even if part of your identity is as an "outsider," being taken seriously, at least by voters, is a requirement in politics.

From my first conversation with Andrew over coffee in 2017, we'd had a goal of reaching the debate stage—it's what everyone thinks of when they consider presidential elections. For us, it would get our message out there to as much of the country as possible, and theoretically to have that message taken seriously enough to move the needle on policy. If we could just stand next to these other candidates such as Joe Biden, Bernie Sanders, Elizabeth Warren, or, heck, even John freaking Delaney, it would be a game changer for us.

And, sure, every campaign defined legitimacy differently, but I did know one thing: if you *didn't* make that debate stage, you were *not* a legitimate contender for the presidency. Millions of Americans would tune in to the first debate in June and make their assessment as to who was legitimate by looking at who was on the stage.

Unfortunately, once again, to get the legitimacy of the debate stage, you needed . . . legitimacy. At the time, the rules about what a candidate had to do to qualify for the first debates hadn't been officially announced, but historically, while they'd been all over the place, all debate qualification rules required some level of "legitimacy," as defined by either various networks holding the debates or the DNC, typically including some combination of polling and fundraising numbers: in 2016, for instance, qualifying for the first debate required polling at 1 percent or better in at least three separate polls.

You can see why *not even being listed in the polls* was a pretty serious problem for us.

Legitimacy was a wall we kept banging our heads against, and we celebrated even the tiniest signs that we were making a crack in it. In October 2018, the same month we were left out of the *Politico* article, FiveThirtyEight ran a feature called "Who's Behaving Like a 2020 Presidential Candidate," with an extensive list of those they regarded as making up the potential Democratic primary field based on things like visits to early primary states, inclusion in polls, and other "presidential" activities. Their initial list of some thirty possibles didn't include us, but we did get a mention in the article: "I'm keeping an eye on businessman Andrew Yang," the writer said. "He could run at least a semi-serious campaign."[4] Semi-serious! We'll take it! We were seriously fucking *elated*. I slapped that quote on the wall next to our "longer-than-long-shot" poster. Shortly after that, a number of outlets started occasionally referring to Andrew as a candidate for president, including CNN and Fox News. The mentions were rare, and we didn't make it onto any fancy grids, but occasionally we'd sneak into a full list of who was running.

In early 2019, as we discovered the power of podcasts, memes, and math, our growing popularity allowed us to hope that our legitimacy problem would start to disappear.

But while we were big on the internet, Andrew Yang still wasn't considered a "real" candidate—one worth taking seriously—by most mainstream outlets or voters. An "interesting figure," but not someone that most experts who talked or wrote about presidential politics for a living thought of as more than a footnote— if they thought of us at all.

There was no denying that our decision to focus on reaching *our* people, not rich people, was working. Potential voters were identifying with Andrew Yang, and we had the numbers to prove it. Web traffic, email sign-ups, social media followers, dollars raised, and number of new donors—all were on an upward tra-jectory. But unless we solved our legitimacy problem, there would be a low ceiling on our candidacy. On the flip side, if we could make Yang a legitimate candidate, the sky was the limit.

We needed to find a way to use our newfound popularity to do more than just make a few little cracks in the "legitimacy" wall that was keeping us out of the game—we needed a crack big enough that we could use it to break the whole thing wide open.

And exactly two days after Andrew's appearance on Joe Rogan's podcast, we found it.

On February 14, 2019, the DNC announced the brand-new requirements for 2020 Democratic presidential candidates hoping to qualify for the national debate stage:

> *Democratic candidates may qualify for the first and second debate by meeting one of the two following sets of criteria:*
>
> - *Polling Method: Register 1 percent or more support in three polls (which may be national polls, or polls in Iowa, New Hampshire, South Carolina, and/or Nevada) publicly released between January 1, 2019, and fourteen days prior to the date of the Organization Debate . . . Any candidate's three qualifying polls must be conducted by different organizations, or if by the same organization, must be in different geographical areas.*
>
> - *Grassroots Fundraising Method: Candidates may qualify for the debate by demonstrating that the campaign has received donations from at least (1) 65,000 unique donors; and (2) a minimum of 200 unique donors per state in at least twenty U.S. states.*[5]

In non-politicospeak: get 1 percent in three different polls *or* get one dollar from a whole bunch of people around the country, and you can debate on the national stage.

Just like that, we had our crack. Our target to aim at.

Andrew called me: "Whatever we're doing, stop doing it, unless it helps us get to 65,000 donors. I want anyone and everyone who has ever touched this campaign to know this is our one and only priority."

So I marshaled our now eight-person team at our headquarters in Manhattan: "Drop everything. The only thing that matters between now and early June is getting 65,000 people to donate to our campaign. Only thing. No exceptions."

I ended my impromptu presentation to the staff by quoting Stephen Covey: **"The main thing is to keep the main thing the main thing."**

This decision turned out to be one of the best we made in the entire campaign, and it is a tactic we used over and over again.

The lesson here is one that is vital for all longshots. Almost by definition, being a longshot or a newcomer means you have limited resources. Say you're launching a new product: What are the odds you can have the highest quality, the lowest price, the widest distribution, the fastest delivery—all at once? Part of the rationale behind identity branding is focus. The goal isn't to identify the longest possible list of strengths; it's to identify your unique strengths, the few areas where you offer something different, and to authentically focus on those. This focus isn't just important in defining who you are and how supporters can identify with you; it's just as important in deciding what you *do*.

The question is always: **What is your most important goal, and what is the one thing that would do the most to move you toward it? How can you use your strengths to make that one thing happen?**

Figure that out, and then focus your energy there.

In other words: *Keep the main thing the main thing.*

This sounds so simple and cheesy—but way too many people miss this and get distracted by unimportant variables that don't matter. For instance, what their competitors are doing, what feels good, or what they think they should be doing based on the way things have always been done.

To our surprise, after the new debate criteria were announced, other candidates polling at our level (0–1 percent) kept focusing on the traditional path to legitimacy—cable news appearances, meeting with local elected officials, holding big-donor fundraising events, begging for endorsements, and so on. This seemed foolish to us. None of these things did much to either increase the number of individual donors or move the polling numbers in a meaningful way, at least not quickly enough to meet the deadline (which was two weeks before the first debate in June). Maybe these other candidates, many of whom were sitting senators, representatives, or governors, assumed their polling would rise. Maybe they thought the money would pour in. Or maybe they just didn't change their approach because it didn't occur to them to stray from what was established. But we had already learned that lesson:

Ignore what's established; focus on what works.

Frankly, the hardest part is ignoring the emotional feelings you get by staying on the beaten path. It feels *good* to go on cable news. It feels good to find an elected official, expert, or political organization to endorse your campaign. But once the main thing is clearly defined, what feels good doesn't matter. **What actually matters is what actually works to get you there.**

In the words of Andrew Yang, if we made the debate stage, the world would ask, "Who is that Asian man standing next to Joe Biden!?" And we would be in the game. You could no longer compare Andrew to the Free Hugs Guy. He would be a real, legitimate candidate for president of the United States.

And getting there didn't require endorsements. It didn't require mainstream cable news hits. It didn't require millions of dollars. What would work to get us on the debate stage was getting 65,000 people to each give our campaign one freaking dollar.

This was right in our wheelhouse. And after a year of emailing *Politico* reporters and pollsters, hoping for the best, it was a relief to have something tangible to do with a clear, guaranteed threshold for success.

So we hustled.

We focused the burgeoning Yang Gang and all our energy onto one task: Get as many people as possible to donate one dollar to Andrew Yang.

You like Yang? Don't just talk about it, donate one dollar.
Oh, you want to volunteer? Awesome: get ten friends to give one dollar.
Your organization would like Andrew to come speak at an event? That's great! Get
everyone to donate a dollar and we'll talk.

We made the barriers to donate to our campaign as low as possible. We took our (limited) newfound riches post–Joe Rogan and spent them on highly targeted Facebook ads with quick clips of Andrew dropping policy knowledge using: "DONATE $1 TO GET THESE IDEAS ON THE DEBATE STAGE" as the call to action. We built a progress bar on our website with a little animated Andrew Yang who moved forward every time someone donated any amount—slowly but surely heading toward our goal of 65,000 donors.

Digital Ads. Volunteers. Memes. Podcasts. Repeat. Yang Gang superfans would check in daily with little accomplishments like "I got twenty people to give a dollar today at the supermarket!" or "My mom, grandma, brother, sister, father, and both uncles have all given one dollar!" Many joked that they would wake up to check the status of the progress bar like it was Christmas morning.

The little animated Andrew Yang moved farther and farther across the progress bar on the home page, closer and closer to our 65,000-donor goal . . . and pretty soon, people outside the Yang Gang started to take notice.

Like Sam Stein, a senior politics editor for the Daily Beast. He saw that we had 47,000 donors on our progress bar and were averaging over 2,000 additional donors every day—and he wrote an article covering our strategy.

How Little Known Andrew Yang May End Up on the 2020 Debate Stage by Gaming the System

You've probably never heard of him. And yet, he's about to bust through the DNC's debate entry threshold.[6]

He posted the story on March 7.

We officially qualified for the first debate on March 12, 2019. Exactly one month after Andrew's Joe Rogan podcast appearance.

What. A. Moment.

After a year of hustle, and stress, and dumb ideas, and MATH signs, and podcasts, and speech prep, and begging for money, and learning, and failing, we had done it. Our little army of political misfits had shocked the world. Andrew Yang was going to take his ideas onto the presidential debate stage. To put this in perspective, Kirsten Gillibrand, a senator from New York with a multimillion-dollar war chest, did not qualify until *three months* after us. (In late May, her campaign finally put an individual donor tracker on their website to encourage supporters to prioritize getting to 65,000.) Other candidates I love—Senator Cory Booker, former HUD secretary Julián Castro, Governor Jay Inslee, Governor John Hickenlooper—also qualified well after our "longer-than-longshot." It was both slightly hilarious and deeply vindicating to see the cable news graphics of "qualified" candidates at the time—the list included Joe Biden, Bernie Sanders, Elizabeth Warren, Pete Buttigieg, Kamala Harris, and . . . wait for it . . . ANDREW FUCKING YANG. Yup, we'd finally made the grid.

We'd spent months being laughed at in nearly every major city in the country, trying to sell a vision to people who weren't in the market for one. And it wasn't just rich strangers who weren't interested: I lost friends after I joined the campaign—or at least discovered which friendships were based only on our shared work or social circles. Many people who were eager to hang out when I worked on Wall Street were suddenly less responsive. Even our families weren't always exactly confident that dropping everything to work on this campaign was anything short of crazy. We *knew* we were onto something, but most of us never got much validation.

So, on the one hand, I wanted to give the world a triumphant middle finger and crow *WE WERE RIGHT!!! Andrew Yang IS the real deal. These ideas ARE worth talking about. Automation IS actually happening. People DO care about this.*

But on the other, bigger hand, I was overwhelmed with gratitude; I wanted to cry tears of pure joy. Even writing this gets me emotional. I went to an expensive, big-name college because I thought it would give me a better chance of making a difference, then took a Wall Street job so I could pay for that decision, and started a nonprofit and worked in philanthropy to do what I could while getting out of debt. I had always felt called to devote my time and energy to something bigger than me—because I think whatever advantages you have should be used for *good*, not just to benefit yourself. I'd finally left Wall Street to take a real crack at making real change, at doing something that mattered, and to see this vision matter to other people—tens of thousands of them so far—meant more than I can say. The Yang campaign felt like it was my reason to freaking exist.

It's happening, I remember thinking. *It's really happening. Andrew Yang is taking off.*

On March 19, 2019, one week after we qualified. *Vanity Fair* ran an article titled:

"YANGMENTUM: ANDREW YANG DRAWS THOUSANDS IN SAN FRANCISCO"

I blew it up and put it on the HQ wall, of course.

———————

The high of making it to the debate stage was so energizing that it only made us work harder—the campaign was pedal to the metal for the next two months. Hell, the Yang Gang was so excited that they kept up their push for one-dollar donations.

We increased the progress bar's goal to 100,000 donors, then 120,000—and kept hitting it.

By mid-May, in the course of three months, we had:

- Gone from thousands of followers to hundreds of thousands of followers online
- Built a national volunteer army with chapters in every major city
- Hosted multiple thousand-person-plus rallies in a dozen cities nationwide
- Raised nearly $2 million from more than 100,000 donors
- Grown from five full-time staffers to more than twenty
- Established three new offices in Iowa, New Hampshire, and South Carolina
- Been featured on every major cable and digital news outlet
- Outpolled more than fifteen established elected Democrats and
- Qualified for the first two DNC national debates

And we had done all of this with no experience. The average age of the staff was twenty-six. Every day was an exercise of making decisions we had never made before and reacting to the consequences in real time.

But we proved that experience didn't matter, because this was a new game, with new rules.

And simply put, what allowed us to finally be considered legitimate is the fact that **the game has changed.**

Traditionally, legitimacy was "bestowed upon you" by the powers that be. And the gatekeepers of political power were not interested in our no-name outsider talking about robots and looking to give everyone $1,000 a month. Frankly, if we'd run for president eight years earlier, many of the tactics we used during our path to the debate stage and legitimacy would never have worked. But some twenty-first-century game changers let us use our strengths to get around the traditional established path.

We've seen this impact our lives in thousands of different ways outside of politics—our ability to connect online has disrupted the balance of power and made it easier for longshots and outsiders to break through in nearly every industry. Artists and musicians can build businesses or get discovered from anywhere. Giant industries can be disrupted by new ideas that fundamentally transform the marketplace. Fan communities can even resurrect cancelled television shows. People can organize, discover, normalize, and innovate on larger scales and in less time than ever before.

Politics has been slow to catch up. But—as Bernie Sanders and Donald Trump proved in 2016—it's not immune to the impact of these changes. The DNC had learned their lesson; they knew the game had changed and added a grassroots donation pathway to the debate requirement in an attempt to evolve.

Here's a breakdown of the old game versus the new in politics:

The Old Game: "Traditional Gatekeepers"	The New Game: "21st-Century Game Changers"
Mainstream Media Traditionally, you need your candidate to get as much attention as possible from big newspapers, websites, and radio and TV news outlets. You also want them appearing personally on as many as possible—CBS, ABC, NBC, Fox, MSNBC, and CNN—ideally in prime time. Plus, you hope that popular political hosts and commentators speak about your candidate regularly, as these outlets craft our national political narrative(s). Many call this "earned media." FiveThirtyEight tracks candidate "mentions" on major news outlets—among debate-qualified candidates, we were always last or close to it.	*Alternative Press and Social Media* Podcasts. YouTube. Social media. Memes. This is where more and more people get their news and information today (and where the vast majority of young people do). A formal communications team that develops relationships with major media outlets is important, but far less so when your candidate can go directly to Twitter or Instagram Live to make a statement. Play well in this space and you don't need mainstream media to cover you anywhere near as much.
Surrogates and Endorsements These include the leaders of the DNC and RNC, local party chairs, large unions or special interest groups (NRA, Emily's List, Planned Parenthood, etc.), and of course, local/state/federal representatives and senators. They generally have powerful donor and supporter bases, and they can sway the press and public opinion by endorsing certain candidates. And (in addition to your candidate appearing on mainstream news shows), various "surrogates," whether members of the above groups or other experienced politicos, might be invited to speak on air to sing your candidate's praises or defend his or her positions. Their credibility "validates" your candidate.	*Celebrities and Influencers* Getting Elon Musk, Dave Chappelle, or Donald Glover to endorse you (as we eventually did), or speak on your behalf, is in many ways more powerful than having a former senior advisor for the John Kerry campaign acting as a surrogate. A tweet from Chance the Rapper earned us more articles and impressions than an endorsement from the vast majority of elected officials, union leaders, or organizing groups would have. Except for the very biggest names, people in political positions of power often lack the ability to cut through the noise of today's attention economy, which means their ability to sway voters has massively diminished.

The Old Game: "Traditional Gatekeepers"	The New Game: "21st-Century Game Changers"
High-Dollar Donors In 2018, there were 91,718 individuals who gave the maximum donation to a political candidate.[7] Aside from the obvious usefulness of their funding, these individuals are also often well known to the political establishment, and their opinions carry a lot of weight. Money talks, and these folks have the ears of every political gatekeeper alive. As of March 1, 2019, we had fifty-four individuals give the maximum donation to our campaign, and the *vast* majority had never given to a presidential candidate ever before.[8] Safe to say, we were not a player in this space.	*Small-Dollar Donors* Instead of trying to get the maximum amount out of the usual max donors, we used the internet to go after literally everyone else without breaking the bank. Plus, if a small-dollar donor gives even a small amount once, they are likely to give again. By the end of the campaign, we had over 400,000 individuals donate to our campaign, an average of around $35, and more than 75 percent gave more than once. In fact, thousands of our supporters gave so many small-dollar donations that they ended up hitting the maximum amount! Another plus is that small-dollar donors typically give online and not at fancy fundraisers, which saves you time and money.
Large Campaign Apparatuses and Political Consultants Once you have money and influence, you can finance a large team of staffers to build and maintain relationships with all these power brokers. Hiring a $50,000-a-month consultant with experience working with successful candidates or campaigns was usually good for a press article or two, and it "legitimized" you in the eyes of the traditional power players. We had no political consultants and had a very small and inexperienced staff at the time.	*Nimble Campaign Apparatuses* Instead of building an expensive team and relying on traditional power brokers to continue funding you, twenty-first-century campaigns can hire staff as their support scales up. In other words, they don't put the cart before the horse. Many call this "bootstrapping" in the entrepreneurial world, and it's effective in multiple industries, politics especially. I can't tell you how many 2020 presidential candidates struggled or dropped out because they had to pay for a massive staff in early states and/or expensive consultants, and fundraising didn't keep up. Heavy overhead has very low correlation to success in the twenty-first century, and particularly so in a long presidential primary.

Now don't get me wrong—the traditional sources of power are still hanging on. For instance, the DNC was still in charge of the rules for who made the national debate stage. And you can find hundreds of examples where the political establishment is still thriving, especially in local races and primaries where the average human is not paying attention and turnout is small. Eric Adams won the New York City Democratic mayoral primary with minimal social media presence, no celebrities or influencers, and very few small-dollar donors. On the contrary, he lined up many of the traditional political endorsements, high-dollar donors, mainstream press, and a union political machine behind him—kicking Andrew Yang's ass in the process. Lots of donors and social media followers do not necessarily equal lots of votes (more on all of this, and the mayor's race, later).

Simply put, the argument that the establishment is dead or ineffective is wrong—it's just no longer the only way to do things. The mainstream political gatekeepers were beginning to show their cracks, and we were exploiting them to achieve national relevance.

I recorded an audio note to myself at the beginning of June 2019: *"We got an unknown man, with no experience or connections, onto the debate stage to be president of the United States. I'd be even happier if I wasn't so exhausted."*

Every member of our team was basically vibrating with excitement. What we'd accomplished was truly incredible. *Wait until the world hears our message on the debate stage,* we thought.

At the same time, we were at a level of mental exhaustion none of us had ever experienced. We worked sixteen-hour days and seven-day weeks. We ate pizza and terrible delivery Chinese; drank shitty beer at night if we had a free moment. Many of us were living on the road, to and from cheap Airbnbs in Iowa, New Hampshire, and South Carolina. I started grinding my teeth at night.* Tempers got a little shorter. Conversations got a little more tense. The stakes were higher than ever, and everyone knew it.

---

* The dentist made me get a freaking night guard, which is miserable—don't grind your teeth, folks!

The game had changed, and we'd leaned in to our unique strengths and stayed laser focused on the variables that mattered to take advantage of that opportunity.

But, while we had qualified for the national debate stage by playing a different game than the rest of the field, our twenty-first-century tactics could only take us so far.

Eventually, we still had to actually fucking debate.

5

AUTHENTICITY OVER ALL
Letting Yang Be Yang

Andrew Yang appears without a tie during Democratic debate, and people have some feelings
—Yahoo! News headline

OUR STRATEGY FOR THE FIRST DEBATE WASN'T VERY COMPLICATED. HELL, IT WAS barely a strategy. It boiled down to this:

Get Andrew the microphone.

I know, I know. But, in our defense, we believed we had a powerful message that would carry us through on its own merit.

The other politicians onstage could fight over the usual Democratic talking points; when it was Andrew's turn to speak, he would explain the fourth industrial revolution, and the need for a universal basic income of $1,000 a month. He had done this effectively countless times now on some huge national stages, like Stephen Colbert, and his own CNN Town Hall just the month before. Plus, Yang was a master at marshaling facts and statistics to make his points, and he'd been a debate champion in high school. Surely *some* of those skills would apply.

Except they didn't. Because a presidential debate is not an actual debate. It's a beast. A massive production that we did not fully understand.

The first DNC debate was held in Miami, Florida, and hosted by MSNBC. Twenty candidates had qualified, so the debate was split into two nights, with ten candidates per night. By the luck of the draw, we got slotted into night two, where most of the front-runners—Joe Biden, Bernie Sanders, Pete Buttigieg, and Kamala Harris—had also been placed. We felt like we'd made the A Team; everyone would be watching, and we were pumped for the opportunity.

Pumped . . . but comically underprepared.

The Miami Beach Convention Center, where the debate was being held, was decked out like this was the NCAA men's basketball Final Four—which I guess it kind of was, except this was for political junkies. Huge three-story signs reading "2020 DEMOCRATIC PRIMARY DEBATES" hung from the front and side walls of the building. Police barricades and light-up traffic signs directed people to various areas, and supporters of each candidate lined the roads in their respective swag/merch/T-shirts, holding huge signs and chanting—I later learned that some teams had three or four approved chants they were allowed to use, and that was it. Literally some teams were so prepared they had a campaign staffer script the damn chants.

Inside the main auditorium was the stage and seating for a couple thousand people. Most of the seats were "given" to DNC donors and officials (making for the most establishment-y audience in existence), but every campaign got ten to thirty seats (how many varied from debate to debate) for their own guests (who were instructed not to wear any campaign paraphernalia or cheer for their candidate, just applaud politely). Many campaigns used the debates as a fundraising tool: "Raise $10,000 for the campaign and get a debate ticket!" We had not done this. Not because we were morally against selling political favors—we just didn't think of it.

In addition to the main auditorium, there were greenrooms (again: not green). Each candidate got their own room in Miami, and all were located along one long hallway, so there was a constant parade of staffers and candidates, with everyone sizing up everyone else.

"Oh, Amy Klobuchar is carrying three suit options, I wonder which color she'll go with?"

"Beto O'Rourke certainly brought a lot of staff with him."

"Tulsi Gabbard has a legit military security guard. Did you see that?"

I'd eventually get to know a number of the staffers on other campaigns, but in Miami, no one knew what to make of the Yang campaign yet, so I mostly got strange looks. We weren't sure how many staffers to bring to Miami, and out of fear of not having enough, we essentially brought everyone on our twenty-person staff. Besides, it was tough to exclude anyone, given it was all we had talked about for months.

Since Miami was a big convention center, each campaign also had a decent-sized workroom—these were basically the war rooms for campaign staff. Since Miami was our first, I chose to watch the debate in the greenroom with a couple other staffers, but the workrooms were usually a place for staff to watch the debate and work on their rapid responses—live tweeting, texting reporters, and preparing for whatever our press "spin" would be after the debate.

Which leads us to the "spin room," which can best be described as a massive clusterfuck. This is where campaigns and candidates go after the debate to literally lie about—sorry, "spin"—what happened during the debate. It's essentially a free-for-all for reporters to access presidential candidates following the national spectacle. They always seem to keep the room *ice* cold, possibly to keep everyone awake during the long hours of reporting following the debate. It's always a huge room with high ceilings—usually a convention center floor or college stadium/gymnasium—and covered in host-network debate logos. The mainstream cable news outlets (think MSNBC/CNN/Fox/ABC/CBS) have all purchased formal TV desks and camera setups, which are lined up around the perimeter, and in the middle, the "regular" or "lower-budget" reporters (think digital reporters from Vox, Telemundo, Business Insider, etc.) run around chasing whoever walks in. It's oddly not as loud in there as you'd think, as everyone wants to hear what candidates are saying. You enter through a long, barricaded walkway, with reporters stacked on top of each other on either side to shout questions at candidates as they pass by . . . most candidates just keep walking.

Once you're past that barricade, you're thrown to the sharks. Some candidates get completely mobbed—especially if they've had a good performance. One night there were so many reporters trying to get a piece of Andrew and Elizabeth Warren shaking hands that Senator Warren fell into her staffer and nearly toppled off one of the press risers. On the flip side, if you're deemed irrelevant to other activities in the room, the press literally ignores you. For instance, if you're a "regular" candidate, and you arrive when none of the front-runners are around, the press makes you the center of attention, surrounding you with cameras and microphones; then a big-name candidate like Harris or Warren walks in and the press vanishes—leaving you standing there like the kid no one wants to pick for their dodgeball team. Andrew called this getting "big footed" by another candidate, and while it can happen anywhere on the trail, it was especially painful in the spin room with every reporter on the planet present.

So that's the world we were suddenly dropped into for the first time in Miami—but aside from all the hoopla and craziness that comes before and after, there is also, of course, the debate itself.

The key to a good presidential debate performance, especially with a large field, is to somehow get everyone to pay attention to you. It's the attention economy squeezed onto one stage. Sometimes you're the front-runner and the spotlight comes to you naturally, so your job is to make sure that spotlight is positive, and that you defend yourself well. This was Joe Biden's job at essentially every debate.

Sometimes you're the challenger, and it's your job to attack the front-runner in a way that brings the spotlight back to you. This was usually everyone else's role.

Other times, you're the focus of a national news story, and that makes you a target in some particular way, and your job is to defuse that bomb—an example is Pete Buttigieg, who later that year got some bad press about his handling of the police department as a first-year mayor. He'd been rising in the polls, and the story broke right before a debate, so we all knew that everyone was coming for him; sure enough, he fended off attacks all night.

No matter what, though, ten candidates onstage at one time during a two-hour prime-time debate makes for a complete shitshow. The whole thing becomes a circus, with candidates jockeying for airtime and the best one-liners and zingers, hoping it'll be the lead story in the news and post-gaming that follows the show. Each candidate gets sixty seconds to answer a question, and thirty seconds to respond if their name is mentioned. Try explaining a health-care plan designed for three hundred million people in sixty seconds. Now try doing it in a way that people will give a shit about in our attention economy. You end up turning to pithy slogans or sound bites that are void of substance—and the substance was where Andrew really stood out.

Plus, the press wants blood, so the moderators intentionally ask questions less about the issues than about pitting candidates against each other: "Joe Biden, you say we can't afford Medicare for All, but Bernie Sanders says it doesn't matter.

Do you think Bernie's plan is too expensive?" And then it will be a split screen between Joe and Bernie . . . hoping one of them will say something witty to rile up the crowd.

We had a sense of some of this before Miami, of course, but no amount of watching presidential debates can really prepare you for the reality, and I don't think we fully appreciated how challenging the format would be.

So *our* question going into the debate was simple: How can we get our message out there with nine other candidates vying for attention? And like I said, we thought our experience over the last months—Andrew having delivered his message again and again by this point, to so many different audiences—would carry us through. All he needed was his chance to speak, and maybe some extra practice beforehand.

Thus, after a few practice sessions in New York City, the master plan was to fly to Miami and let Andrew take off a few days for family time at his in-laws' house in Palm Beach to decompress from campaign life in the warm weather before getting into prep mode. The day before our debate, we would pick him up, drive him to the hotel in Miami, do some pre-debate press and prep, and then watch the first night of the debates as a team as our final prep session.

So, operating according to plan and blasting Will Smith's "Welcome to Miami" and the AC (it was disgustingly hot, over one hundred degrees), I arrived to collect Andrew from his in-laws. I knocked on the door and, to my surprise, was greeted not by Andrew but by Evelyn, his wife—with a very concerned look on her face.

She then delivered some of the worst news you can get before your candidate's first nationally televised presidential debate: "He's not feeling well."

This was an understatement.

Andrew was horizontal on the couch. In an undershirt and sweatpants. Surrounded by used tissues and toys belonging to his young sons, who were running around the house, one of them screaming. It was obvious that 1) family time had not been the oasis of relaxation we were hoping for, and 2) not only was he not refreshed and recharged, he was sick. *Very* sick.

Now I want to be clear. Andrew doesn't do "sick." He reportedly never took a sick day once in seven years at Venture for America. I'd seen him with a head cold or cough a few times since we started running in early 2018, but these were always minor and over quickly.

I had never seen Andrew like this before. I don't think Evelyn had either.

It was the day before the biggest moment of his professional career (and arguably his life), and he was running a 103-degree fever, looking like he was trying not to throw up, and generally just exuding misery. He also couldn't speak without having a massive coughing fit.

No no no no no NO. This is not happening.

I pulled myself together, and superpositive crisis-mode Zach kicked in.

"All right, man. No worries. Just a little cold! We'll get you an IV, get you some light cough meds, and you'll be ready to rock in no time. It's going to be fantastic. Nothing we can't overcome, baby. The nation needs you! Let's do this!"

I knew Evelyn and Andrew could easily see through my bullshit, but I convinced myself that they appreciated the optimism (despite the looks of annoyance on their faces).

We got Andrew to the car and rode the sixty minutes to the hotel in silence. No more Will Smith. Andrew needed to shower and get some miracle recovery drugs in him stat. A doctor that Evelyn and I found via a quick Google search came to give him an IV bag of fluids and vitamins. It helped a little, but he still looked miserable.

As for how I felt, helpless is probably the best word.

What do you do? Do you change up the strategy? Do you coddle him? Do you play the bad guy and pretend it's all in his head?

None of these options seemed productive. And, honestly, Yang was so sick that it didn't seem like anything I said would have mattered. He was just trying to get through each minute.

The team watched the first night of the debate together, as planned. There we were. On the eve of the day we had been fighting to reach for more than a year—and Yang was lying in bed under the covers, barely able to form a sentence.

We all went to bed that night terrified that he would embarrass himself on national television.

The next day—debate day—I picked up Andrew in his room around 3 PM. I had my game-day blazer and chinos on, and was rocking my lanyards of debate credentials. I've never been a big fan of cable news, but I have to admit, wearing these makes you feel like a badass. I kept all of mine—seven-by-four-inch plastic badges hanging on a cloth lanyard covered with the news-network logo, each reading something awesome like "VIP," "Press," or "Greenroom." I always had access to all three, so I got to wear three at a time—I felt like a manager at TGI Fridays with lots of flair, except in this situation it was cool to wear flair.

"GAME DAY, BABY! How you feelin'!? Ready to rock?" I stormed into his hotel room, Positive Zach back in full effect.

Andrew still looked like death. I just kept talking, walking him through a few talking points and logistics and various loose ends before the debate started.

"Zach," Andrew interrupted sternly after about ten minutes of my one-sided rambling. He was struggling to breathe. "Please be quiet. My biggest concern is not having a massive coughing fit onstage."

I paced the room in awkward silence as he finished getting ready. My nerves were running a mile a minute. In his state, he had managed to get his suit pants and dress shirt on, and his garment bag was laid across the bed, with three different color necktie options draped over it.

Looking to be helpful and channel my own nervous energy, I picked up his tie options from the garment bag and held them up for him to examine.

Andrew had never worn a tie on the campaign trail. Ever. Not even during his recent CNN Town Hall. But there was a general understanding that we would put one on for the debate stage. We had discussed it as a team beforehand: a tie would look presidential, and appearing at the debate was partially about being seen as legitimate. It's the biggest job interview in the world; a tie was a sign of respect for the job. Besides (of course I looked this up), no male presidential candidate in modern political history has debated without wearing a necktie.

But now, Andrew looked at me, looked at the ties, and rasped, "Honestly, I freaking hate those things. And restricting my airway out there feels like a terrible idea right now."

The "no-tie" option we'd dismissed suddenly came roaring back, and the pros and cons ran rapid-fire through my head. I mean, it wasn't like people would think it was a gimmick, because like I said, he'd *never* worn a tie on the campaign trail. And there was a chance that being the lone male candidate with no tie would help him stand out on the crowded stage, reinforce his identity, and get people interested enough to listen to our message. Of course there was also the chance that people would hate it, think it signified that we weren't serious, and make them take our message less seriously as a result. Or maybe no one would give a shit either way.

I shrugged.

"All right," I replied, and put the ties away, thinking to myself, *Guess we're letting Yang be Yang.*

––––––––––

The networks make you arrive at least two hours early, so once you get to the venue, you're left in your tiny greenroom for what seems like ages with nothing to do but think about what's coming. I paced while Andrew sat in a chair and closed his eyes. My insides were swirling and my hands were shaking. We each went to the bathroom at least three times. Him to cough up a lung. Me just to do *something.*

Eventually, a voice called from the hallway, rounding up the candidates.

I grabbed Andrew—who had not spoken a single word since entering the greenroom—by the shoulders and looked him in the eyes.

"I am so fucking proud of you," I said. "You were born for this. Go shock the world."

"Thank you, Zach," he said softly.

Jesus, take the wheel, I prayed as he walked out ahead of me.

The candidates were lining up in the hallway leading to the debate stage in podium order. They all looked wound tight with nervous energy. Their staff members, who stood against the hallway walls alongside them, all looked as antsy as I was.

Some of the first words spoken came from Eric Swalwell, congressman from California:

"You didn't wear a tie!?" he exclaimed to Andrew. "Ah, that's awesome! Nicely done." He sounded kinda jealous.

Privately, I gave myself a small fist bump.

Eventually all of the candidates were in line—except one.

Now, I'm not just saying this because he ended up as president. Honestly, I didn't think Joe would win the primary. But I will *never* forget watching Joe Biden make his entrance into that hallway.

He waltzed in like he owned the world, shiny gray hair pristine, trim and energetic, his navy-blue suit perfectly fitting and pressed—looking like a god-damn silver fox. Not a glimmer of nerves on display. He might have been heading off to crack some beers with his friends, not be attacked by nine hungry political challengers in front of nearly twenty million people. He walked up to every single candidate and shook their hand, looked them in the eye, and gave them a warm

Andrew Yang, me, and Andrew Frawley where it all began: in Yang's mom's apartment. Muhan Zhang took the photo; otherwise, he'd be perched on that pile of boxes next to me.

Our first campaign event at our new NYC headquarters.

Andrew signing our campaign
wall in HQ. It was pretty bleak
for a while. But then again,
so was our campaign.

Our initial campaign team!
Left to right: Andrew Frawley,
Andrew Yang, me, Muhan Zhang

Me, Andrew, and Carly Reilly
at an event in Iowa, Fall 2018,
long before most people in Iowa
cared that we were in Iowa.

Selfie in our shitty campaign van full
of boxes in November 2018, with Carly
and a few staffers behind us. The boxes
were full of MATH signs, A/V equipment,
and Andrew's platform. (Literally.
We'd packed a makeshift stage.)

Our official *Joe Rogan Experience* photo. (Note the button with our "abomination" of a logo.)

This was the "get Andrew to the debate stage" progress bar on our website. Little bitmoji Andrew moved across the bar and jumped up and down when we hit our goal.

GET ANDREW INTO THE DEBATES

65,000 individual donors needed by May 15th, 2019

65,083

DONATE

65,000
DONATIONS

Andrew backstage outside our not-at-all-*green*room at the first Miami debate.

Also from the Miami debate, Andrew doing a walkthrough before the live event . . . I can still literally *feel* how sick he was.

An example of the incredible signs and art that the Yang Gang created. Someone gave Andrew this massive thousand-dollar bill at our first LA rally.

This was our second LA rally, the one that I described in the introduction. LOOK AT THAT CROWD!

Don't worry. If Andrew couldn't debate for some reason, I was on standby.

Andrew at his second debate in Detroit, July 2019. What. A. Glow. Up. When I'm done with politics, I'll become a stylist at GQ with this photo as my portfolio.

Me and Andrew navigating the spin room after the Ohio debate in October 2019. You can see the sharks—I mean mobs of reporters.

Some of the road team celebrating hitting the 4 percent polling threshold that would help us qualify for the December 2019 debate. From bottom left, clockwise around the table: HaiTao Wu, Lacey Delayne, Don Sun, Andrew Yang, me, Randy Jones, Erick Sanchez, Jermaine Johnson, Michael Hoeppner, Ethan Dunn, Jeremy Frindel.

Andrew and me eating turkey legs at the Iowa State Fair in 2019. The press obsessed over what the candidates ate and Andrew happily obliged . . . by eating everything.

Probably my favorite photo from the trail. Andrew celebrating his birthday at a campaign rally in Iowa.

Never mind. I lied. This is my favorite. A screen grab from our all-day "Ask Me Anything" livestream on Halloween 2019. The campaign wall looks a little different here, doesn't it?

Me next to our super-sweet campaign bus. Reminder: we used to travel in an unmarked white van full of boxes.

hello with that classic pearly-whites grin. Man, he could not have been smoother. And I worked on Wall Street in client services—I *know* smooth.

Now that's a politician, I thought. Everyone else in the hallway was thinking it too.

Then it was showtime, and all ten candidates were escorted to the wings of the stage, single file, by MSNBC staffers with clipboards and headsets. The candidates were not allowed back this way until after the debate, so when the big double doors closed behind them, they were officially out of their staffs' hands, and there was an audible (and, in my opinion, hilarious) sigh of relief from the thirty or so staffers in the hallway. We'd basically sent our kids off to the first day of school: Once the bus pulled out of the neighborhood, all we could do was wait for it to be over (and hope we'd all make it through in one piece).

I headed back into the greenroom to watch the debate on the small TV there, along with two other senior staffers. I tried to remember to breathe as Andrew was announced and walked onstage, waving and halfheartedly smiling through his fever.

Immediately, as if on cue, MSNBC anchor Brian Williams quipped: "Andrew Yang, would it kill you to throw on a tie?"

And just like that, #AndrewYang was trending all over the internet before the debate had even officially started.

#AndrewYang is not wearing a tie! What a badass!

#AndrewYang is not wearing a tie! How disrespectful!

Some people (including most marketing experts) loved it for being completely on brand. Other people (including most political pundits) hated it for disrespecting the office. But whether they loved it or hated it, they were talking about Andrew Yang—and he hadn't said a word.

Which was good, because the words he did say, once the debate started . . . well . . . his performance was objectively pretty rough.

Andrew answered just a couple of questions—all poorly. The first question he got should have been a gift: The moderator mentioned Andrew's plan to give every American $1,000 a month (sadly, the closest anyone, Andrew included, would get to explaining UBI all night) and asked how he planned to pay for it. Andrew launched into the topic of value-added tax; the moderator followed up by asking whether his plan, then, was to give people $1,000 so they can "spend that $1,000 on value-added tax," and Andrew responded by talking about how value-added tax increases buying power—it was all wonky, boring, and did nothing to make his case for UBI, or even to make it clear what UBI really *was*. The only other questions Andrew answered all night were the ones they asked every candidate—he said a couple of sentences, total, about China and climate change. He didn't speak again until his closing statement, which was a generic statement about how he was the best candidate to beat Trump. Over the course of the two hours, Yang spoke for less than three minutes (much less than any other candidate by a significant margin), didn't succeed in explaining universal basic income, or his vision, and was in short, completely irrelevant onstage. He looked like he didn't want to be there, which, given his symptoms, was probably true.

It was objectively a terrible performance. I say that with love—most individuals would have fared even worse if they had to attempt a political debate for the first time in front of twenty million people next to nine of our country's best politicians while fighting a high fever and a cough. But still. God awful.

However, as bad as it was, we somehow managed to survive and advance, avoiding *complete* irrelevance and/or national embarrassment simply because—while getting ready to introduce himself on a national stage while miserably sick—Yang felt more comfortable without a tie.

Yup, Andrew's tielessness saved us.

I don't know how to prove this, but I'm confident that Andrew's words-spoken-onstage to words-typed-in-postdebate-press-coverage ratio set a new world record. We legitimately owned a press cycle after the debate without really saying anything, as shown by these headlines:

"Democratic Debate 2019: Andrew Yang's Bold Lack of a Tie" (*New Yorker*[1])

"Andrew Yang went for a casual look at the Democratic debate, leading Brian Williams to ask 'Would it kill you to throw on a tie?'" (Business Insider[2])

"Presidential hopeful Andrew Yang's 'missing tie' has its own Twitter account now" (CNBC[3])

"Andrew Yang appears without a tie during Democratic debate, and people have some feelings" (Yahoo![4])

"Andrew Yang goes (GASP!) tie-less on Democratic debate stage" (*USA Today*[5])

Andrew's postdebate "story" was all about the tie, rather than his actual performance. And because that lack of a tie was true to his identity, it communicated something authentic about who he was (however semi-accidentally). Our supporters latched on to it as something positive to take away from our underwhelming debate performance, and we even gained some new interest and attention.

In short, it gave us a second chance. Despite dropping the ball, we were still alive and somewhat relevant in this race.

And now we had a giant problem . . . and very little time to solve it.

There were four weeks before the second debate in Detroit, Michigan. And while, yes, being sick was a large part of the fiasco that was the first debate, and at times it did feel like MSNBC cut Andrew's mic, and they absolutely didn't ask him enough questions—the reality is that these debates were not a format that suited Andrew well. They rewarded traditional politician behavior, which we had spent the past year and a half avoiding at all costs.

However, they were also the only way to talk to tens of millions of Democratic primary voters at once. We *had* to get our message to cut through during a hot mess of a nationally televised debate. There was no workaround or innovative strategy we could muster up to avoid it.

We had built a strong campaign from an operations standpoint: we functioned efficiently, prioritized the important things, and had outperformed expectations up to this point. But the bar to qualify for the fall debates would surely be higher than it was for the first two, and if our next debate performance was as bad as the first, not only would we not grow our support the way we needed to in order to stay in the game, there's a good chance we'd lose a lot of the support we had.

All roads to the presidency went through the national debate stage. But on the debate stage, we were not presidential material, and Andrew and I both knew it.

Detroit was where we would deliver our message and make our case to continue as a contender in this election—or fall by the wayside as a tieless also-ran.

We only get one shot. Cue Eminem.

So when we got back from Miami, I found myself in Andrew's Hell's Kitchen apartment one Saturday morning, asking our candidate a very blunt question: "Do you actually want to be president of the United States?"

Andrew had his glasses on and wore a wrinkled graphic tee with a pair of faded Levi's. His hair was worse than usual; he was still slightly sick.

"It's cool if you don't want to be president," I clarified. "Seriously. If you hated that debate so much that you'd rather just make this a book tour, and you're happy focusing on getting these ideas out there without really competing as a candidate, that's okay. We've accomplished more than anyone ever thought we would. On a personal level, I feel proud to have come this far, and you should too. We can just accept that we're not politicians and be satisfied that we rattled the cage a little bit and call it a day."

Andrew stared back quietly.

"But if that's the goal, the staff needs to know it. And so do I. Right now, we're all playing to win. Who knows if we can, but we think we have a chance."

I continued.

"*However* . . . if you *do* want to win, if you're all in, then let's be all in. That means prepping like a fucking fighter for the next debate. It's going to mean us pushing you, hard, and you letting us. It's going to mean every day we leave everything on the field. So that at least if we bomb in Detroit, we can say we gave it our all."

Andrew was still just looking at me, soaking in what I was saying. Finally, he spoke.

"Yes," he said. "I am all in."

We talked a while longer, and as I was about to leave the apartment, he stood up to stop me.

"Hey, Zach." He walked up closer and put his hand on my shoulder. "There is no worse feeling in the world than feeling that you let people down. You and the entire team have given so much to me."

He paused to collect himself.

"I just want you to know that it means everything to me." His voice was breaking as he fought back emotion. "And I won't let you down."

———

I meant what I said about cueing Eminem. "Lose Yourself" was the theme song of the month that July. I played it every morning on my way to debate prep.

Because, yes, every day was debate prep—all day, every day.

We'd started by clearing Andrew's calendar. His *entire* calendar. No rallies, no trips to primary states, nothing. Yang was not leaving New York City until the Detroit debate—with one exception: the first week, the week of the Fourth of July. He got the whole thing off. This was my call. You can't train if you're still exhausted from battle. We had been fighting for a year and a half, and he was still rebounding from the sickest he'd been in a decade. He needed to recover and rest.*

We'd then blocked out the following three weeks for debate prep. We had to get dramatically better at debating . . . fast. And for that we needed bigger guns. So, for the first time since the campaign started, we hired a political consultant—specifically, we hired a debate coach, along with a professional speaking coach.

Once prep began, I quickly learned how little of political debating is about having good answers to the questions. Heck, half the time it seemed like the most important skill a politician could have was *dodging* a question. There are a lot of questions that there is just no way to answer thoughtfully in sixty seconds. A poorly-phrased answer can be clipped to make you look like an asshole; a rambling one to make you look clueless. And after hours and hours of drilling questions, you start to see how talented (or terrible, depending on your perspective) journalists can frame an issue so that no matter what you say, you're toast. The thing is, Andrew was so logical and policy focused that he always wanted to *actually answer the question* (gee, what a novel idea). Unfortunately, unlike in his high school debating days, having the best argument doesn't always get you very far—for one thing, there's usually no way you'll have time to make it. What's more, when you only get five to ten minutes to speak, total, over the course of a two-hour debate, you have to use every opportunity to hammer whatever core message you are trying to get across. This was, after all, our biggest chance to get our ideas out there and taken seriously.

So Andrew learned how to pivot away from certain questions, and how to connect his answers back to the message he wanted to drive home. We wrote and practiced answers for most major political topics, and the debate coach gave Andrew a triangle framework for his message that made it easier to get back to—for instance, he could answer a question in one sentence, then segue into automation statistics (leg one), talk about the need for universal basic income (leg two), and normalize the idea by noting that Martin Luther King Jr. suggested it in the 1960s (leg three).

---

* And yikes was *this* a controversial call. *Guess what, team? We just bombed a debate, and now it's time for vacation!* But honestly, it was the only option, and if there's one thing I've learned about leadership, it's that a lot of the job is making unpopular decisions and sticking to your guns when your team pushes back. It's important to listen to your team, but if you're the one with the responsibility—credit for the good and blame for the bad—you have to be able to make the tough calls. This was one of those.

He learned to use the legs in any order, and how to transition to one of the three no matter what the question was. He also learned to end any statement with a quick, compelling close—an important skill in a situation where you were always in danger of running out of time.

Debates, however, are not just what you say, but *how* you say it. So debate prep also meant teaching him a different type of delivery—one designed for sound bites and political punditry. Andrew practiced professional speaking techniques for hours, watching videos of himself and of great orators, doing weird exercises like speaking with cork in his mouth, and practicing his answers while doing a variety of physical movements to bring out the energy.

We drilled content and delivery, nine hours a day, for fifteen days straight.

All that said, it's one thing to answer questions with me and a few coaches standing in front of you. It's another thing entirely to do it in front of a three-thousand-person audience, with the klieg lights in your face, debate-timer lights going, flanked by professional politicians who have a vested interest in embarrassing you as quickly as possible, in front of twenty million people including everyone you know and love and have ever met. Debates were a massively nerve-racking feat, and our guy had only one rep under his belt—during which he was more focused on not having a coughing fit than performing well.

We needed to simulate a real debate.

We started with the venue: We rented out an auditorium in Times Square with a greenroom (still not green), a grand entrance, and a way to re-create many aspects of the real debate. Next step was an audience, so we invited one hundred of our closest supporters—some early donors, friends, family, and Yang Gang members. They *weren't* allowed to bring their phones into the auditorium (this was for our eyes only); they *were* instructed to be relatively hostile to Andrew (the establishment audience did not cheer for him in Miami). Then we got lights. Music. Moderators.

The only thing missing was the other debaters . . . so we hired professional actors to play Bernie, Kamala Harris, Biden, and the rest. They all learned their lines, looked the part, and had obviously done their homework—in fact, they were eerily good, and substantially more intimidating than any of our staffers could have been.

Our mock debate was scheduled for six days before the real thing, and we were excited to see the results of our weeks of intensive prep. We did everything by the book: Andrew showed up ninety minutes early, went to his greenroom to wait, and when it was time, walked out into the hallway to join the other nine "candidates," all lined up single file, just like in Miami. The debate theme music played, the lights came on, our moderators introduced everyone, and we began the debate.

Only to discover that—after all our practice and the money spent on consultants and the building rental and actors—Andrew was . . . not very good.

He had made massive improvements from Miami. But he still wasn't breaking through on the crowded stage. Like, at all.

He was stiff and mostly monotone. He was robotic. He didn't smile like he normally did. And he certainly didn't insert himself into the main action of the debate. He was simply focused on getting his lines out—which he did, but without any of the Andrew Yang gravitas and confidence we were all used to seeing in his appearances by this point. Remember, this was almost six months into the era of Andrew Yang as superstar—he'd commanded the stage at huge rallies in front of thousands, traded banter with late-night hosts, hosted his own CNN Town Hall with grace and style. Now, it was almost like we'd gone back in time, to the wooden, TED Talk–giving Andrew of a year ago.

If he gave a performance like this in six days, the campaign was dead in the water. No question about it.

Panic set in.

"He's not *Yang*!" I yelled to our debate team afterward (which included Matt, our two newly hired consultants, and a few other senior staffers), wanting to bang my head against a wall. "It's so strange. Any other prime-time setting—Joe Rogan, the town hall, the freaking South Carolina fish fry—he slays! But during his biggest moment—"

"This is different," our debate coach interrupted me. "Two completely different beasts. You can't expect the same Yang from those performances and these."

We kept arguing. Back and forth. Mainly on what to tell Andrew. Should we tell him he'd sucked? Or should we tell him he'd greatly improved? He *was* better than he'd been in Miami, and we didn't want to risk shattering whatever confidence he had. On the other hand, he couldn't improve what he didn't know was a problem.

This argument went on for *way* too long. At least twenty minutes. With Andrew standing outside the room, waiting for us to finish deliberating and review with him.

Finally, we brought him in. The room was quiet as he entered.

"Hey, guys." Andrew broke the painful silence. "I didn't think it was *thaaaaat* bad?" He laughed awkwardly. "I actually felt pretty good. What do you think?"

I led with what we'd decided was the best approach for his confidence.

"Hey, man, you made massive improvements," I began uncomfortably, "but we've got a long way to go before the debate, and we gotta keep working on some things."

Andrew looked at us blankly in silence.

"You know," he began, slowly, "it's a really shitty experience standing outside in the hallway for half an hour while you all talk about me, and then having to walk in here like I just killed somebody's dog.

"You guys are all in here, talking strategy"—he was speaking a little faster now—"but it doesn't seem to make sense to have these review sessions without me, your best player." His voice was getting louder. "Actually, I'm not just the best player, I'm the entire team. In fact, I'm the only player on THE FUCKING FIELD!"

And we're off.

"WHAT THE FUCK IS THAT ABOUT? You guys are worried about my performance—*'What are people going to think!? What are people going to think!?'* ARE YOU FUCKING *KIDDING* ME? IF ANYONE HAS ANY SKIN IN THIS GAME, IT'S ME!

"What's the WORST THING that happens to YOU GUYS if I bomb in Detroit? You get to put on your résumé, *'Oh hey, yeah, ha ha, I worked for this shithead back in the day.'* WELL GUESS WHAT, GUYS? *I'M THE SHITHEAD!!*"

His voice reverberated off the walls of our small greenroom. It was like we were all standing inside a bell that had just been rung.

He paused, took a breath, and lowered his volume back to his normal speaking voice, though the tone remained stern.

"From now on, I'm included in these conversations. I'm part of the strategy. You treat me like a human being, not some puppet you get to pull the strings of."

We sat there looking at him in what felt like an eternity of silence. It could have been ten seconds or twenty minutes. I wasn't counting. Our debate coaches were *shook*. They had never seen fired-up Andrew Yang.

Finally, I looked over at Matt. And smiled.

"It's nice to have you back, Yang," I chirped.

"Fuck!" he exclaimed, not listening to me. Like he was still putting a cherry on top of the perfect tirade.

But I meant it.

Andrew Yang was back.

Andrew yelling at us wasn't just about him being frustrated. It was him getting his mojo back—and taking control back too. After all, this was *his* vision we were all here working for.

This was him telling us, *Yeah. I fucked up the first debate. But I still willed this entire campaign into existence, and I won't compromise who I am because of one off night.*

And he was right. Damn, he was right.

In the midst of running around Iowa and New Hampshire, and doing press interview after press interview, and hiring more and more people to manage more and more of your life, and more time away from family, and kids, and birthdays, and relationships, and free time, and sleep, and decompressing, we had forgotten the most important thing. The thing that got us here in the first place. The thing that, though we didn't fully make the connection at the time, saved our asses in Miami.

We needed to let Yang be Yang.

We were so caught up in the pressure of appearing on the national presidential debate stage that we'd lost sight of how we'd qualified for the debates in the first place—by leaning in to our unique strengths. We were the Andrew Yang campaign, and for a moment, we'd forgotten the one thing driving every success we'd had: Andrew Yang.

Think about it. Our first big break came with podcasts, where Andrew could express his ideas honestly, without the pressure of national cameras or sound-bite timing. We'd grown our tribe further with memes, by letting him be the anti-politician. And our events got better when we stopped trying to insert scripted moments of excitement and instead went all in on who Andrew really was . . . a numbers nerd (ahem, MATH).

The constant through it all was authenticity—making sure that Andrew was authentically Andrew at all times, even when surrounded by an inauthentic political machine.

Sure, Andrew needed to get better at debating. But trying to make him learn rehearsed answers like a traditional politician was the opposite of authentic, and ignoring what we knew about his strengths and who he was wasn't going to work. We needed to prioritize authenticity over all.

It all clicked after Andrew's outburst, and we leapt into action. We kept the idea of the triangle framework that our debate coach created—but just the framework—and we threw out the scripts. *Let Yang be Yang.* He sucked at reading scripts anyway. The new plan was to let him play around with the phrases and ideas we'd come up with based on what felt right to him in the moment. And we rented another auditorium in Queens the next day, for another day of debate prep—not a full mock debate, but something close enough, with real lights to simulate a TV debate environment.

This time . . . his first answer sucked again, but instead of waiting or giving standard political-expert-type feedback, I interrupted mid-debate, walked up to him, and proclaimed, "Dude. You suck. You look like a robot. You're speaking in a monotone. You have no gravitas. And no one watching thinks you should be president. Here, look." I had recorded him on my phone to prove my point, and now I shoved it in his face and played his answer back.

"See!? It's not you. It's some robot version of you that came back from the future to shittily explain automation, and it's not very convincing."

"Damn," Andrew said with a laugh, watching. "I really *do* suck. Okay, hang on—let me try it again."

We repeated the same question. And just like that, for the first time in our weeks of practice, Andrew Yang the superstar showed up.

Our entire debate team looked at each other as our jaws dropped.

"Yeah!" I screamed, still in shock. "DO THAT. ALL DAY." Pretty sure I was jumping up and down.

And he did. It was like something clicked. He was no longer trying to execute a plan, but was responding to the moderator based on the message he wanted to drive home. He loosened up and started talking more naturally, his voice rising and falling instead of monotone. He occasionally went into robot mode, but when that happened he knew it and fixed it. Humor and laughter started creeping back into his responses, and the feeling of connection with the audience returned. It was like a totally new man had appeared onstage—or not a new man, just one we hadn't even realized had disappeared until he was back.

Authentic Yang was the best Yang. Sure, he wasn't a natural politician. But our candidate being himself was so much better than our candidate pretending to be something he wasn't.

That Friday we stayed in that Queens auditorium all day, practicing with our new and improved authentic Yang.

"All right," I declared, as we were wrapping up our prep session, "if we're going to let you be you, we can't just give you a traditional closing statement. We need to be different—and authentically *Yang*." I thought for a minute. Then I asked: "What's the first thing you think when someone asks you about the debates?"

Andrew paused, and then gave his opinion matter-of-factly. "I think they're a dumb reality TV show and it's a ridiculous activity. We're all up here with freaking makeup on giving rehearsed attack lines. It's not even a real debate."

He laughed. "In fact, even after all the nonsense, all the pundits seemed to care about was the fact that I didn't wear a tie."

And there it was. After about an hour of back and forth, we had the bones of a closing statement, one that perfectly fit our candidate.

Andrew Yang went to Detroit five days later and had what felt like his official coming-out party as a contender on the national debate stage. He ended with this:

> You know what the talking heads couldn't stop talking about after the last debate? It's not the fact that I'm somehow number four on the stage in national polling. It was the fact that I wasn't wearing a tie. Instead of talking about automation and our future, including the fact that we automated away four million manufacturing jobs, hundreds of thousands right here in Michigan, we're up here with makeup on our faces and our rehearsed attack lines, playing roles in this reality TV show.
>
> It's one reason we elected a reality TV star as our president.
>
> We need to be laser focused on solving the real challenges of today, like the fact that the most common jobs in America may not exist in a decade, or that most Americans cannot pay their bills. My flagship proposal, the "freedom

dividend," would put $1,000 a month into the hands of every American adult. It would be a game changer for millions of American families.

If you care more about your family and your kids than my neckwear, enter your zip code at Yang2020.com and see what $1,000 a month would mean to your community. I have done the math. It's not left; it's not right. It's forward. And that is how we're going to beat Donald Trump in 2020.

Authenticity over all. Andrew broke the fourth wall and spoke directly to the voters, called out the debates for their shitty format, and tied it all back to what mattered, his core message of universal basic income. He even got a little joke in there. It was perfect.

Was his whole debate performance perfect? Of course not. We had a lot more work to do, as I'll discuss in the next chapter. But was he solid, confident, and relevant? Did he get his message out? *Absofuckinglutely.* His message was crystal clear to millions of Americans, and our authentic debate close went viral, raising one million dollars from 38,000 people, 34,000 of them brand-new donors. The Yang Gang had its biggest growth spurt since Joe Rogan, and, this time, with traditional Democratic voters. Within a week, we'd qualified for the next debate in September, hitting 2 percent in four different nationally approved polls *and* reaching 130,000 individual donors.

In Detroit, the auditorium and the spin-room buildings were separated by a street. After the debate was over, I ran down that street and waited outside for Andrew.

I'll never forget seeing him walk down the ramp on the side of that empty street.

It was like it all hit me at once. Like this massive wave of relief hit every cell in my body. I almost collapsed from the weight—both of accomplishment and of purpose. I was in tears . . . frankly I couldn't stop crying.

I gave him a huge bear hug. "I'm *so fucking proud of you*, man. You did it. You did it! You fucking did it!"

I've rewritten the ending of this chapter over a dozen times, and every time I cry as I relive it on the page. Call me lame all you want, but in my opinion, if what you're doing doesn't require everything, I mean *everything*, you have, then odds are it's not worth doing. What's the point if it doesn't feel as big as the world, if it's not pushing you to the edge, using every bit of your truest self? Isn't that what we're here to do?

I guess I'll end this chapter by just saying I'm proud.

In the months leading up to that night, hundreds of thousands of people had heard Andrew Yang's message and generously opened up their wallets to support us. Why? Because, I believe, they knew what our team knew: *This message is important. And the world needs to hear it on the national debate stage.* We weren't always the perfect messenger. And we sure as shit weren't the perfect team. But it didn't matter. We were the only messenger. The only team.

And when our backs were against the wall, our entire movement on the line, with one last chance to make our case . . . we delivered.

I will forever be proud of that.

We had a long way to go. But, against all odds, we were still in the game.

6

ADDRESSING THE ELEPHANT IN THE ROOM

The Most Insane Debate Strategy in Presidential History

WE'RE GOING TO GET COMPLETELY LOST UP THERE.

Our debate coach, Edward, passed me a note with that phrase scribbled on it. We were in the middle of yet another mock debate, with paid actors, lights, music, fifty family members/friends of the campaign in the audience—the works, just like before. It was five and a half weeks after Detroit, and the third *real* debate, in Houston, was only six days away.

I know what you're thinking: *You guys are still freaking debating!?*

Believe me, the feeling was mutual. Much of running for president revolves around these horrible debates, but—before you skip ahead—I'm not planning to relive them all in detail. I'm only talking about the debates again here because this third debate posed a different challenge than our first two, and it illuminates an issue that all longshots and newcomers face: irrelevance.

In some ways, this was the same problem we'd always faced, namely: With ten candidates on the stage and Andrew Yang not a front-runner, how do we get noticed?

In the first debate, Andrew's lack of a tie made him stand out from the field. In the second, Andrew finally managed to get his message out, and the uniqueness of that message, along with the fact that, for most Americans, Andrew had been an unknown quantity beforehand, made people notice him.

But for debate three . . . we were clueless.

We'd gotten people to notice our candidate; they knew who he was and what he stood for. Now what? Why should they keep paying attention to him?

Because, with the debate field winnowed down from twenty candidates to just ten, this was a whole different ball game. The ten candidates who'd qualified for the debate and would be onstage in Houston were:

1. Joe Biden
2. Cory Booker
3. Pete Buttigieg
4. Julián Castro
5. Kamala Harris
6. Amy Klobuchar
7. Beto O'Rourke
8. Bernie Sanders
9. Elizabeth Warren
   and
10. Andrew Yang

Yep. It's okay if you laughed. Literally every other candidate on that list was a big name in professional politics. The thing is, only five of these candidates were actually outpolling us—Biden, Sanders, Harris, Warren, and Buttigieg. But every single one had *vastly* more political savvy and debate experience. Houston was the big leagues. And our guy had literally just learned how to play.

Actually, a sports metaphor really is the best way to describe this. Andrew had gotten so much better at debating—seriously, *so much better*—but it was like teaching an athletic adult how to play baseball for the first time. He could hit and throw and run the bases well enough now to be the star of a company softball game, but he was in no way ready for the MLB. How could he be? Unfortunately, the people he was going up against had decades of experience answering questions under fire, with hours and hours of stump speeches and polished political answers to pull from. Yang, in contrast, had a fair amount of practice talking about his core ideas, but he was still learning to master the style-over-substance confines of the debate format; for most topics he had one or two polished answers, many of which we'd only recently come up with. Delivering pithy answers with confidence, thinking on his feet, and engaging in competitive sound-bite ping-pong in front of tens of millions of people was not exactly second nature to him.

And now, in our mock debate—answering questions that we wrote, next to actors who were weaker versions of the real candidates, in front of a small, fake audience—Andrew had just gotten swallowed up onstage. No one felt good.

We went back and forth on what to do:

Me: *We gotta attack! He needs to go for blood! Hammer Elizabeth Warren on her wealth tax!*

Debate Coach: *Have you seen her chew someone out before? Absolutely not, dude, that's a buzz saw we should never send him into.*

Senior Staffer: *Let's tell more jokes! He's better when he's having fun out there.*

Matt: *Yeah, sure, that's just what we need. The internet candidate with more trolling.*

Senior Staffer: *Everyone is talking about guns and school shootings right now. Let's discuss that.*

Andrew: *In other words, use our limited time to address an issue everyone onstage agrees on?*

Me: *We need to just* ignore *the question, and hammer whatever point we want! If they ask about Russia, we just talk about universal basic income and the economy.*

Debate Coach: *Yes, definitely—let's underscore Andrew's lack of experience and make it look like he has no idea how to handle foreign policy.*

At the time, Biden still had a strong lead, polling at almost 30 percent, with Warren and Sanders each looking like serious challengers with numbers in the high teens. Harris was at 7 percent and falling, and Buttigieg was at about 4.5 percent and rising. The rest of the candidates, Andrew included, were all polling at two point something (the debate qualification threshold was 2 percent) and holding steady.[1] The relevance of the five top contenders was obvious. And thanks to their political credentials, the others in the 2 percent club—Booker, Castro, Klobuchar, O'Rourke—were all being covered by the press as relevant; even if the media didn't expect them to win, political reporters wrote about their appeal to Iowa and New Hampshire voters, or their potential to end up on the ticket in the VP position. The press had covered Andrew's message after the second debate because it was new (or at least newly legitimate, thanks to appearing on the debate stage); now the political world already "knew" who he was: *Oh yeah, Andrew Yang—the Free Money Guy. Cool idea, never going to win.*

"What is the perfect debate outcome?" I asked our debate coach.

"Yang's performance cuts through in this crowded field, and the press covers him as a national story after the debate," he replied.

Right. Not happening.

"And what would that get us?"

"We'd raise a ton of money. We'd get a lot of new email sign-ups to grow our email list and volunteer base. And we'd see a bump in polling to help us qualify for the next two debates and continue to grow through the fall."

And there it was. The actual goal.

It was not just to be "relevant," and it definitely wasn't to "win" this debate (the press always declares a "winner"—that was never going to be us). The real goal was to get the *results* that a winner would get. In other words, to see increases in the three metrics our debate coach mentioned:

- Fundraising
- Email and volunteer sign-ups
- Press (driving a poll bump)

Otherwise known as the three cars I described way back in chapter two: money, crowds, and press. Anything that drove these forward would be a win, no matter how we got there.

We got there with something I called the "elephant in the room" strategy.

The elephant in the room, of course, is what everyone is thinking but no one is talking about.

One of the surest ways to break through in the attention economy is to talk about the elephant in the room. If there is no elephant in the room, create one. Then talk about it.

This, again, was not a new technique. Being the first person to address the elephant in the room creates an instant connection with anyone watching—you're talking about what everyone is already thinking! Savvy politicians are good at this. Trump used this to rile up Republicans all the time. There's an issue with illegal immigrants coming to the United States? *We're gonna build a wall!* People hate Washington, DC? *We're gonna drain the swamp!* These were things many folks on the right were thinking, but no one was saying as directly—not only did his supporters love him for it, but the media loved to cover the controversy when he said something shocking. Trump used the elephant in the room to great success in the attention economy.

Democrats used the elephant in the room in their own way in 2020. Before the first debate, there was a lot of talk in the news about Joe Biden's record on civil rights, specifically his efforts to prevent the busing of students to desegregate schools in the 1970s (many on the inside believe that the stories were pitched to reporters directly by the Kamala Harris team). As the leading candidate of color at the time, Kamala Harris called out this elephant in the room during the first debate:

> *You also worked with [those segregationist senators] to oppose busing, and there was a little girl in California who was part of the second class to integrate her public schools and she was bused to school every day. And that little girl was me.*[2]

She knew everyone was thinking about Joe Biden's record on race—and she hammered him on it. Harris's team got an entire press cycle out of this and even made merch to capitalize on the moment. Addressing this elephant bought her a ton of coverage, a fundraising boost, and a bump in the polls.[3,4]

I could give hundreds of examples, but the point is: the elephant in the room can be used in a thousand different ways, depending on the situation.

Andrew and our team were naturally good at this. I mean, you could argue that our entire campaign was about addressing the elephant in the room. *Hey America, while our politicians and media are praising the soaring stock market and our record-high GDP . . . we're literally automating away half of American jobs!*

Plus, we had specifically deployed this strategy while building our identity brand, and to great effect. Our MATH and POWERPOINT merch leaned into the fact that Andrew was a nerdy guy who loved talking about numbers, and it even worked to defang some of the Asian American stereotyping that might have been used against him. Everyone knew he was a nerd—it was the elephant in the room. The MATH hats and "POWERPOINT!" chants called out what no one was saying, turning Andrew's nerdiness into an authentic point of pride, and this confidence made it somehow . . . cool.

So, headed into the third debate, what was the elephant in the room for Andrew Yang?

Basically, it was that he was an afterthought, nothing but "the Free Money Guy." Thus . . .

"Why don't we just get up there and give money away?" I suggested, half joking.

Andrew used to casually make comments along these lines all the time during car rides. "If I'm supposed to be the magical Asian man giving everyone money on this campaign," he'd say, "maybe I should actually do it."

And, in a moment of relative desperation, Andrew's idea suddenly seemed like the most feasible way to stand out on the main-contenders' debate stage. With ABC News giving each candidate a sixty-second opening statement for this debate, we actually had an opportunity to take the microphone and make this magic happen. More specifically, we were suggesting that our candidate, the Free Money Guy, begin a presidential debate in front of tens of millions of Americans by announcing that he would give ten families a chance to see his signature UBI proposal, the "freedom dividend," in action. By giving them each $1,000 per month. For an entire year.

No one loved this idea. In fact, essentially everyone hated it. Which is why I had a hunch that it might work.

To achieve our actual debate goal, we didn't need to attack Elizabeth Warren like a traditional politician. In fact, that tactic had some massive downside risk (getting thoroughly owned by a talented seventy-year-old rival on national TV, for instance). We just needed to make a splash that would drive fundraising, email sign-ups, and press. This would blow up the debate stage and get all the political power brokers to freak out. We could tease a surprise before the debate, build suspense, and then make headlines for days after. Andrew would be *the* story—the coverage would probably not be positive, but it'd be better than being ignored. And even if the media hated it, some voters might not: stunt or not, it was authentic—Andrew Yang wanting to give money to Americans was literally our core message. It would drive huge traffic to our website, as people would sign up for the chance to be one of those chosen. Hell, some of them might like the idea so much they'd donate to our campaign while they were there.

It was ballsy, even for arrogant assholes who thought they could run for president with no experience. Some people even told me it was illegal.*

Now, I'm not completely stupid. I knew the risks. This could make us look like a joke just when people were finally starting to take us slightly seriously. It was possible we'd never recover—campaigns had been torpedoed by less. And while we were never going to be the front-runner coming out of this debate, any great traditional "debate moment" we might have was not going to get covered if we started the night by giving away money from the stage.

But we were the longshot underdog, and in this field of nine political stars, we were basically irrelevant. Expectations for us were zero, and we could use that to our advantage. If Pete Buttigieg made this move, it'd be stupid—he was rising fast based in part on his rhetorical skill, and people were watching him to see proof that an Indiana mayor could handle the presidency. But no one expected anything at all from Andrew Yang going into this debate. He was a likable sideshow no matter what he did. At least with this strategy, he would be owning his lane and authentically addressing the elephant in the room. *If I'm gonna be known as just the Free Money Guy—I might as well give away some money.* He believed in his freedom dividend program; this was him showing just how much, and underscoring that he was about new and actionable solutions, not traditional politics.

It was unlikely we would conquer our irrelevance problem and qualify for the next debates by trying to beat the pros at their own game. This could save our campaign . . . or it could end it.

Andrew and I discussed it the next day.

"One of the rules I live by," he said, "is that you have to give yourself a chance to win. This is risky, but it increases our opportunities to succeed. Plus, it's on message."

It was a go. We were moving forward with possibly the craziest debate strategy in Democratic political history.

---

* This hadn't been done before, and while we believed it was completely legal, there was no way to know for sure what the Federal Elections Commission (FEC) would think. In the end, we decided we were willing to risk being sued. If campaigns can pay DC consultants and Facebook hundreds of thousands of dollars to sway votes but can't give $1,000 a month to people in need to demonstrate a policy in action, well, that was something we were happy to go to court to fight.

The team built a new website landing page to go live during the debate, so that when people went to Yang2020.com, they'd immediately see the entry box—give us your name, email, and zip code to be entered for a chance to receive a freedom dividend of $1,000 a month for an entire year. The day before the debate, I dropped a hint to Sam Stein at the Daily Beast (my new BFF, since he had been one of the first to cover Andrew). He tweeted: "At tomorrow night's debate, Yang will be doing 'something no presidential candidate has ever done before in history.'"[5] His quarter-million followers ate it up, and #YangDebateSurprise was trending nationwide twenty-four hours before the debate was to begin.

On game day in Houston, I was so nervous, I pinned the American flag onto the wrong lapel of Andrew's suit jacket. Yep. You read that correctly. Pinned Old Glory on the right side instead of the left, like I hadn't done this literally thousands of times before. One of my best friends is a Navy SEAL, and he still rides me about it to this day. (For what it's worth, the rest of the debate team didn't catch it either.) I in no way meant to disrespect the flag, but on any other debate night, I guarantee there would have been a Fox News story afterward about how Andrew hates America or is too dumb to know which side the flag goes on. But on this occasion, for obvious reasons, most people didn't even notice.

As we waited in the greenroom (still not freaking green) for the debate to start, we were desperate to distract ourselves from how nervous we were, so we hooked up an iPad to the TV and streamed Beyoncé's Coachella performance. To be honest, it actually helped . . . the marching bands were badass. And if Beyoncé could perform like that right after having a baby, we could survive pissing off some politicos, right? Sadly we couldn't pretend to be at Coachella forever—soon enough, Andrew got the call to head to the stage, and we all moved to our workroom to watch.

Julián Castro was first up. He delivered his sixty-second opening statement. Amy Klobuchar was next, then Beto O'Rourke, then Cory Booker. And then it was Andrew's turn. He looked straight at the camera and started to speak:

In America today, everything revolves around the almighty dollar—our schools, our hospitals, our media, even our government. It's why we don't trust our institutions anymore. We have to get our country working for us again, instead of the other way around. We have to see ourselves as the owners and shareholders of this democracy rather than inputs into a giant machine.

When you donate money to a presidential campaign, what happens? The politician spends the money on TV ads and consultants and you hope it works out. It's time to trust ourselves more than our politicians.

That's why I'm going to do something unprecedented tonight. My campaign will now give a freedom dividend of $1,000 a month for an entire year to ten American families, someone watching this at home right now. If you believe that you can solve your own problems better than any politician, go to Yang2020.com and tell us how $1,000 a month will help you do just that. This is how we will get our country working for us again, the American people.

An awkward murmur, with a few scattered cheers, rolled across the auditorium, but those on the stage looked as if a flash grenade had just gone off in front of them. I had never seen a group of professional politicians break character so fast.

Pete Buttigieg, Mr. Polished, was supposed to be the next speaker. But Senators Amy Klobuchar and Kamala Harris burst into laughter. Senators Bernie Sanders and Elizabeth Warren gave the camera "WTF?" looks. No one really knew what to do. The audience, which was full of DNC donors, was half-laughing, half-confused AF. The crowd murmur grew distractingly loud. Everyone in the room was looking around, as if to confirm what they just witnessed with those around them.

"Mayor Peter Buttigieg?" the ABC host, George Stephanopoulos, prompted, trying to restore order and move on through the opening statements.

Buttigieg seemed to take a minute.

"It's original, I'll give you that," he said.

At that moment our entire campaign team erupted in cheers.

Everyone was off their game. It was like you could see a collective thought bubble over the auditorium:

Andrew Yang just interrupted the debate and gave away a bunch of money! Can you do that!? What an asshole! But I kinda love it? What is going on!?

Andrew stood at his podium, looking completely unfazed as the other candidates struggled to regain their composure. Slowly, the debate arena returned to relative normalcy, and the debate continued as usual.

But the internet was a different story.

We blew up.

Like, we *thought* we had blown up before. But that was peanuts. This was a whole new level.

But first, let's talk about the collective discomfort from the traditional pundtry. Because it was glorious.

Here are some excerpts from a few of the commentators recapping Andrew Yang's debate performance for the *New York Times*:

> The "I'm giving away $1,000" gimmick made me yearn for the future debates that he won't qualify for. (David Leonhardt)

> In the last debate, he was memorable for his discussion of the robots and mechanized labor that are taking jobs from human beings. Last night, he dropped the robots and simply offered voters cash. It was unexpected and comical to his opponents, who openly laughed. (Melanye Price)

> Andrew, the Democratic debates are not a game show with you supplying the grand prize. (Mimi Swartz)

In general, the traditional gatekeepers that I outlined in chapter four reacted exactly as expected. Mainstream media, surrogates, elected officials—they virtually all dismissed us (see the *NYT* comments above) or laughed at us outright (see the other candidates' reactions, also above). High-dollar donors . . . well, there were plenty laughing at us in the audience that night, and none of them were beating down our door with a check right afterward. As for political consultants and traditional campaign professionals, let's just say that literally no one (except our debate coaches—thanks team!) thought this was a good idea.

Hell, even the Yang Gang was calling for my head. Here are a few comments from the YangforPresidentHQ Reddit:[6]

> This feels far too REALITY TV for me to feel comfortable with.

> That's the exact wrong way to introduce America to the concept of UBI. Comes off as a gimmicky contest [rather] than a serious intent to resolve certain economic inequalities.

> If this is really his "surprise," it's absolutely pathetic. He wants to hold a fucking lottery for a monetary giveaway at the presidential debate? He's going to get torn apart for this because it displays a shocking lack of empathy and is all about self-promotion. What a clown.

But internally, we knew we had nailed it. And a few days later, we got to announce that in the seventy-two hours after the debate, the Andrew Yang campaign had:

- Raised over $1 million in average increments of $30 each;[7]
- Received 450,000 email address sign-ups;[8]
- Trended worldwide on virtually every single social media platform, with "Andrew Yang" the fourth most searched topic in the world that evening;[9]
- Gained more Twitter followers than any other candidate;[10] and
- Had ten million visits to our campaign website, three times more than any other candidate.[11]

Yup. The *New York Times* called us a gimmick. *And it didn't matter.*

Because here's how our twenty-first-century campaign strategy played with some of the "game changers" I outlined in chapter four:

- **Alternative press and social media:** We went viral. The giveaway broke out of traditional political coverage and made news with outlets like MTV, *Hollywood Reporter, Fast Company,* and more, and Andrew Yang was trending on literally every single social media platform on the planet. We got so much new media coverage that traditional media outlets *had* to cover us, giving us more headlines than any other moment on the campaign.[12,13,14,15]
- **Influencers and celebrities:** Alexis Ohanian, the founder of Reddit (and husband to Serena Williams), offered to match our freedom dividend donation. Hundreds of other celebrities shared our giveaway moment and/or the link to enter with their followers.
- **Small-dollar donors:** We raised a million dollars almost immediately and now had 450,000 new people to email for donations.

Our newly improved name ID was no joke, and it went way beyond the usual audience for politics. "Andrew Yang" had more web mentions the night of the debate and over the three days that followed than nearly any other human being on Earth. From then on, not only could he not go anywhere without being recognized, he would get mobbed on the street. Suddenly, Andrew Yang was a beloved international celebrity. (Who doesn't love a guy giving away free money, I guess?)

We felt vindicated by these responses, but what happened next surprised even us: namely, the old-school political gatekeepers got over their hate . . . *fast*.

Three days after the debate, after we'd announced our massive email and fundraising haul, CBS News, *Politico*, Yahoo!, RealClearPolitics, MSN, and the *Wall Street Journal* all wrote glowing articles about our strategy.[16] *The Daily Show*, *Jimmy Kimmel Live!*, *The View*, and dozens of other popular shows began clamoring to get Andrew on the air. (And yes, the Yang Gang got behind our strategy, too, once they saw that it worked—thank you, Yang Gang!)

We were no longer in danger of irrelevance. In short order, we'd qualified for the next debate in November, and raised a shocking $10 million in the third quarter. For context, this was more than three times what we'd raised in the quarter before, and it dwarfed the third quarter totals of many of our more established opponents, like Cory Booker, who raised $6 million. Hell, we raised almost as much as Kamala Harris, who raised $11.6 million—and 99 percent of our donations were under $200.[17]

Now you may be thinking: *Yeah, Zach, your marketing gimmick was a success in the short term, but you guys didn't win, and it was because of moves like this. This marketing stunt was your candidacy in a nutshell.*

And maybe you're right.

But before you dismiss our third debate strategy as a mistake, let me outline a few important points that narrative misses:

1. Our team had a theory that the traditional gatekeepers in politics were becoming more and more irrelevant. We knew that this strategy would be massively effective in standing out on the debate stage, and we were betting that even if the traditional gatekeepers hated it, the influence of the twenty-first-century game changers would outweigh that. And we were right—what surprised even us was that it didn't just outweigh the influence of the traditional political types, it actually *overruled* them, and they changed their story.

2. Gimmicky or not, this move was more than just a stunt—it was authentic and on message. Andrew's argument, the reason for his candidacy, was that our country is in crisis and that the most important piece of the

solution involves implementing universal basic income as soon as possible. What better way to demonstrate both the seriousness of his belief and the impact of his proposed solution than by putting our money where our mouth was on the biggest stage in American politics?

3. What else should we have done? Andrew was simply not going to light up the debate stage at that point, with that field. Anyone who says we would have broken out with a more traditional debate play is wrong and seriously underestimates the extent to which we were ignored and dismissed, day in and day out, and how hard our campaign had to fight for every scrap of attention we got. I am 100 percent confident that our message alone would not have cut through during the debate or been covered afterward. Without this move, there is a very significant chance that we wouldn't have qualified for some of the subsequent debates, making our campaign, and movement, dead in the water in the fall of 2019. We prioritized short-term results because without them, there would be no long term.

4. You can't argue with those short-term results. I can list twenty-three other legitimate candidates who would have killed for the money, press, email list, and awareness we gained from this move. After the Houston debate, Andrew Yang was a household name known *because* of his signature policy, the idea we'd been fighting to get into the mainstream every single day for a year and a half. We've covered all of this already, but it's hard to overstate—this *made* us. It made Andrew a contender in a way he literally never had been before.

But *ZACH!* you're thinking. *At what cost!?*
Which brings me to . . .

5. Don't forget, it was September. We still had the October, November, December, and January debates at which to shape public opinion before primary voting started. That's an *eternity* in politics. And if you disagree, let me remind you that Kamala Harris "won" the June debate and surged to second in national polling throughout the month of July 2019. Four days after the Houston debate in September, Andrew Yang was outpolling her in her home state of California.[18] She dropped out of the race two months before primary voting began.[19]

To stand out in a crowded field as a longshot and a total outsider, we knew we needed to do things differently. The plan was to lean in to our unique identity and build an army of supporters who identified with us, gain legitimacy by making it to the debate stage, use that platform to introduce our candidacy and our message, stay relevant however we could, and then grow from there. Broadening our appeal as a serious candidate later in the fall seemed feasible. For one thing, Andrew is brilliant and had more to offer than just UBI—once people were paying attention to us, the depth and substance he'd showcased on podcasts might actually get a chance to shine. For another thing, not only was he improving his debate skills all the time, but expectations for us were massively low. If Andrew went from a C– to a B+ on foreign policy at the next debate, people would give him an A simply because they expected so little.

To sum up, the attention economy being what it is, we knew that we had plenty of time to change the narrative going forward, if we played our cards right.

Every arena—politics, technology, art, retail, the nonprofit sector, whatever— has its own norms and its own level of tolerance for those who stray from them. Not only does that tolerance vary by industry, it varies over time and according to a million other factors. You make the best decision you can based on the information you have, but whether it will turn out to be the right one isn't always possible to predict. Honestly, while I can concede that some of our attention-getting tactics hurt us later in the race, I can only concede that in hindsight.

At the time, here was our reality after Houston:

We had millions of dollars to spend. We were rising in the polls. And we had qualified for two more debates—two more opportunities to make our case to American voters.

And a couple of weeks after the debate, CNN was covering us like this:

Yang, who officially launched his presidential bid in 2017, was an after-thought in the Democratic field until recently, largely dismissed by his Democratic opponents and party operatives. But Yang has rallied a coalition of liberal Democrats, libertarians and some disaffected Republicans around a series of distinctive policy positions, namely his so-called Freedom Dividend, a plan to give every American adult $1,000 a month universal basic income that Yang argues would alleviate a host of social ills and eradicate poverty.[20]

The same article said that our grassroots fundraising had "turned the once longshot candidate into a fixture on the debate stage who is now polling better than most of his Democratic competitors."

Once longshot.

Suddenly, we had become a top contender for the presidency of the United States.

So much for getting lost up there.

INTERLUDE

I THINK IT'S IMPORTANT TO PAUSE HERE AND REFLECT ON WHERE WE ARE IN THIS STORY.
It is October 1, 2019, and Andrew Yang is now a bona fide national superstar. We're raising hundreds of thousands of dollars a day in thirty-five-dollar increments, we're wanted on every local and national news outlet and entertainment platform in the country, and CNN had just called our candidate "the hottest 2020 candidate this side of Elizabeth Warren right now."[1]

On a personal level, there was a healthy "mission accomplished" feeling, at least for myself and the early team members. We had gotten the message out there. Andrew Yang was a THING. Despite all the people who'd laughed at us, despite every obstacle thrown our way, we had done it.

And frankly, I thought that we would go on and win from here. Many on the team, especially those who'd been there from the beginning, felt the same way.

I know that sounds ridiculous, particularly in hindsight, but if you think about it, in some ways the hard part was over. Going from a nobody to a serious contender in the amount of time we had is next to impossible. So many things had to go right—if you did manage to do it, it was because you had the right message and messenger.

We felt Andrew was the right guy. We knew he had the right message. Hundreds of thousands of people agreed with us, and their numbers were growing every single day! Our campaign was an avalanche that could not be stopped! This was a movement of the people, and we were inspiring a revolution that would save our nation and defeat Donald Trump!

Yet . . . we lost. Badly.

In fact, we never grew much beyond where we were on October 1.

Sure, we raised more money, and more and more people fell in love with Andrew Yang. In fact, our millions spent on TV advertisements in the early states of Iowa and New Hampshire increased our favorables (just what it sounds like—the percentage of poll respondents that view you favorably versus unfavorably) to some of the highest in the field.[2]

But this enthusiasm was never reflected in the polls that truly moved the needle—when people were asked who their first choice for president of the United States was, Andrew Yang was not at the top of their lists.

On October 3, 2019, Andrew Yang was polling at a 3.8 percent average according to RealClearPolitics. He essentially stayed at that level for the rest of the 2020 Democratic primary, peaking just shy of 5 percent near the end of January 2020. He got 8,914 votes in the first round of voting in the Iowa caucus (5.1 percent); once the caucus process was complete, he wound up with 1 percent of state delegate equivalents, for a distant sixth-place finish.[3]

In New Hampshire, which had been our strongest state, we lost all momentum after our Iowa result, and we went on to receive 8,315 votes (2.8 percent), finishing in eighth place—behind Tulsi Gabbard and Tom Steyer, candidates we had consistently outpolled throughout the race.[4]

So what happened?

How did you blow this, Zach!?

I imagine a healthy number of you are thinking this. Or were at the time. I sure as hell was.

But hindsight makes a few things clear.

We lost . . . but we didn't fail. No one "blew" anything. We didn't win, but we had an *astonishing* level of success for a nonpolitical nobody. Our campaign didn't put Andrew Yang in the White House, but it put his ideas on the national stage. We ran a campaign that we should be proud of, and we built a movement that is still going strong. The future of Andrew Yang, universal basic income, and his ideal of a human-centered economy is bright.

Another thing that hindsight makes clear is this: realistically, we were never going to win this election.

Sucks to read that, right?

I didn't know that when we started, or even in the fall of 2019. I believed with every fiber of my being that we had a shot.

But looking back, it was never—believe me, *never*—going to happen. We were a longer than longshot, and while we shocked the world and smashed through even the most generous expectations, we still had a massive deck stacked against us.

I strongly believe that elections usually boil down to big-picture rather than small-picture factors: Obama won because he represented change when Americans were desperate for it. In some ways, Trump won for the same reasons—he tapped into a rapidly growing part of the country that felt left behind, and to whom Hillary Clinton represented those in power who were to blame.

Why did Andrew Yang lose?

We lost because he was a risky person to vote for, an outsider with big (and, to many, scary) ideas and no political experience, running in an election where the majority of Democrats were terrified and wanted the safest bet to defeat Donald Trump and restore order to a government and institutions that seemed to be crumbling.

It wasn't because we didn't knock on enough doors (we probably didn't). It wasn't because Andrew dropped too many f-bombs (he probably did). It wasn't because the media was biased against him (they definitely were). And it wasn't because his campaign team was too inexperienced (we definitely were). These hurdles didn't help, but it was impossible to overcome the macro factors. We say the game has changed, and it clearly has, but not enough for Andrew Yang to beat Joe Biden. We're not there yet.

All that said, there is still value in reflecting on what happened and what we could have done better. Both to understand how to navigate our newly disrupted political arena in the attention economy, and to understand how to navigate the challenges of being a longshot in other arenas. Because the truth is that the bar is higher in politics than in most fields. For one thing, as I'll discuss more in the next chapter, risk tolerance is lower in politics than in many other areas. For another, you can have massive success in most industries without getting the kind of national support a presidential victory requires. If we hadn't been the Andrew Yang campaign, but instead a new nonprofit, with our goal not the presidency but rather building a movement and a foundation to forward the cause of UBI, our campaign and tactics would clearly be considered a massive success.

Our campaign definitely wasn't perfect—or even particularly close to perfect. We struggled with our lack of experience and "learning on the job." We struggled to handle our campaign's rapid growth and to adjust as conditions changed. We didn't always find the right balance in terms of when to heed traditional wisdom and when to trust our entrepreneurial instincts. Most importantly, many of the things we did to launch a strong brand that people could identify with, and to grow our base quickly, prevented us from leveling up the way we needed to later on. Virtually all of these issues are relevant to any longshot in any arena.

So as our story continues over the next few chapters, I'll reflect on some of the less-sunny stretches of our adventure. The times we didn't light the world on fire. The times we faced impossible decisions, or realized after the fact that we'd made the wrong ones. And more importantly, what those episodes mean, both for the future of this movement, for political brands in general, and for anyone trying to compete and build a lasting influence in the new attention economy. The rest of this book will talk about what happened after we took off—the mistakes we made, what we learned, why it matters, and most importantly, where the heck we go from here.

7

WHAT GOT YOU HERE WON'T GET YOU THERE
The #YangMediaBlackout

I am running for president because, like so many of you in this room, I'm a parent. I am a patriot. I have seen the future that lies ahead for our children, and it is not something I'm willing to accept.
—Andrew Yang, Iowa Liberty and Justice Celebration, 2019

I STOOD BACKSTAGE IN AN ARENA PACKED WITH MORE THAN TEN THOUSAND PEOPLE in Des Moines, Iowa. It was November 1, 2019, and we were at the Liberty and Justice Celebration—previously known as the Jefferson-Jackson dinner, a cattle call for all Democratic presidential hopefuls held a few months before the state's early February primary. This is where candidates traditionally kick off their final push before caucus voting begins; it's where Barack Obama's impassioned speech in 2008 gave him a major polling bump that laid the groundwork for an Iowa victory and a viable path to the presidency.

Andrew was in the middle of a speech that we hoped would be our version of Obama's 2008 game changer. We had spent the past week perfecting it, and he was nailing it.

This was our rebranding moment. Our moment to level up.

Or at least, that was our vision.

We were currently in fifth place in the field, and just a few weeks past announcing our highly unexpected $10 million third-quarter fundraising haul. Since September, our inexperienced and ragtag team had evolved to include a number of seasoned DC political professionals. Their experience ranged from overseeing ad strategy for the Bernie Sanders campaign, to creating targeted communications that helped Hillary Clinton win the nomination in 2016, to running and analyzing polls for hotly contested Democratic congressional campaigns, to building digital operations for major progressive nonprofits across the country. Our new-found popularity and resources allowed us to take our operation to the next level, and we were in serious contention mode. Now we just had to take our candidate to the next level as well.

Our freshly assembled political team had looked at the data and the primary landscape and determined that Andrew was likable, but no one was ready to vote for him for president. At this point in the race, most of the country viewed him as a new, interesting, maybe even exciting political figure. We had name recognition at last (77 percent nationally), and our "favorables" were generally positive, with 40 percent of Democratic voters having a favorable opinion of Andrew, and only 15 percent having an unfavorable view. For context, we were the seventh most-liked and the second least-disliked candidate in the field.[1] Our worst data point, by far, was on the question of whether Andrew "possesses the right experience to be president of the United States"; just over half of voters did not believe he had the experience needed. He was the free money and/or automation candidate. He had a die-hard base of supporters, but he'd need much broader support to be a serious contender.

With four months before the Iowa caucuses, our plan was to shift gears to build that support, showcasing a different side of Andrew Yang. So less talking about automation and $1,000 a month. If you were into that, you already identified with our campaign. We now had the difficult challenge of overcoming the perception that Andrew wasn't experienced enough for the presidency, which of course was an uphill battle, given that he was legitimately inexperienced in the political world, *and* that his outsider energy and new perspective were viewed as an asset by many current supporters. Frankly, if you were looking for the "experience" candidate, you could literally pick anyone else in the field.

Our compromise solution was to work to build a deeper relationship between voters and Andrew Yang the human being, attempting to broaden our identity brand. We couldn't make Andrew more politically experienced in four months, but we could counter his lack of experience by allowing voters to identify with him as a person (not just a candidate) enough to trust he had the judgment to make up for it. In 2008, Obama—at the time viewed as an inexperienced candidate himself—did this well. Hillary Clinton ran a TV ad called "3 AM." It featured shots of children sleeping, a red phone on a desk, and a voice-over that said, "It's 3 AM and your children are safe and asleep. But there's a phone in the White House and it's ringing. Something is happening in the world." The ad ended with the question, "Who do you want answering the phone?" showing Hillary answering that late-night call, making a direct contrast between her experience as secretary of state and Obama's lack of foreign policy experience.[2] In response, Obama flipped the scenario right back on her, using it as an opportunity to emphasize his judgment and trustworthiness as a human to put voters at ease around one of his biggest weaknesses as a candidate. "When that call gets answered," his response ad stated, "shouldn't the president be the one, the only one, who had judgment and courage to oppose the Iraq war from the start, who understood the real threat to America was al Qaeda in Afghanistan, not Iraq . . . In a dangerous world, it's judgment that matters."[3] He countered lack of experience with judgment and trust. Voters found themselves identifying with Obama, visualizing him getting a phone call regarding a global emergency and thinking: *Frankly he seems to be pretty trustworthy; I'm okay with him answering the phone.*

For us, it was time to emphasize parts of Andrew's identity we hadn't leaned in to much: his thoughtful intelligence, his deep conviction and sense of duty, the roots of his campaign in his concerns as a patriot and a parent. The human side of Andrew Yang.

After nearly two years of trying to get the world's attention, we finally had it. This speech in Iowa was our chance to demonstrate that Andrew was more than the quirky tech guy with big ideas, that the country's problems weren't just a puzzle for him to solve—they were personal. He was a serious candidate with a deep purpose behind his run, worthy of being taken seriously.

We all worked hard on the speech, combing over every line. Each candidate got a full twelve minutes to speak; finally Andrew would have a chance to address a traditional political audience without being beholden to the debate format or trying to gimmick his way to relevance. Andrew took his preparation as seriously as he had for the debates, and he spent hours rehearsing his delivery.

In the days leading up to the event, our newly improved communications team called every reporter we could find, briefing them on our new messaging and pitching them our leveling-up story:

This will be a new Andrew Yang.
When he delivers the speech of the night, believe me, you'll want a feature on his new direction.
Andrew Yang is about to demonstrate that he is a serious contender for the presidency.

As I stood watching Andrew onstage in Des Moines, I was feeling good. CNN's chief political correspondent Dana Bash had followed us the entire day. Weezer's Rivers Cuomo had performed at our predinner rally, and we'd marched—with more than one thousand Yang Gang members from all over the nation—from our pre-event concert to the event stadium. And then, Andrew had taken the stage and delivered some of the most confident and powerful public speaking I've ever seen from him.

I'm running for president because of a thought that the parents here in this room have had but we've been afraid to express.
And it is this: our kids are not all right.
They are not all right because we have left them a future far darker than the lives we have led as their parents.

If you Google "Andrew Yang Kids Are Not All Right Iowa," you can find the full speech; it remains one of my favorite moments from the campaign trail. Even the sound engineers standing around me were impressed, and they gave Andrew enthusiastic high-fives as he walked off the stage.

My phone blew up with texts from other campaign staffers and reporters:

Best speech of the night.
Wow your boy came to play tonight.
Who is THIS Andrew Yang!? Very presidential. Well done.
I cried. This was incredible.

I was ecstatic. *We did it!* I thought. *Speech of the night! A surprising, serious, and impressive Andrew Yang! Every reporter will write this story—how could they not??*

Except . . . they didn't.

There were no dream headlines like, "Andrew Yang's New Direction Makes Him a Serious Contender in Iowa" or, "Andrew Yang Makes a Powerful Pitch to Parents after Iowa Democrat Dinner."

There were no headlines at all.

Heck, forget headlines, Andrew Yang's name was not mentioned once in the *New York Times* recap of the event.

He wasn't mentioned in the *Washington Post* either. Or on NPR. Or in the *Wall Street Journal*.[4] CNN was the only mainstream outlet to mention him in their coverage of the event, and even then it was just a brief paragraph.[5]

Generally speaking, if you were not one of the ten thousand people in that stadium in Des Moines, Andrew Yang might as well not have attended one of the biggest political events of the Democratic primary.

Welcome to the #YangMediaBlackout.

Now look, our campaign had struggled to get media coverage since day one. You know this already—I've griped about it plenty over the course of the book, and I've talked about how it influenced our strategy in the attention economy where caring is rare. But what I haven't mentioned is that, at some point in 2019, as Andrew started rising in the polls, the lack of coverage became so blatant that it wasn't just our own team complaining—the rest of the world started noticing as well. The Yang Gang called this the #YangMediaBlackout. And while the internet tends to overhype and exaggerate, this was very, very real. Some press outlets like the *Guardian* even covered this phenomenon—ironically, covering Andrew Yang by covering the fact that they were not covering Andrew Yang (I know, very meta).[6]

As an example, take ABC's on-air coverage of all the candidates from January 1, 2019, to August 31, 2019—a period that includes our campaign's surge in popularity, Andrew's surprising qualification for the June and July debates, the June debate's no-necktie moment, the July debate that introduced him to America, and his qualification for the September debate. Here's what those totals look like for the ten candidates who qualified to appear in Houston in September:[7]

Joe Biden—68 minutes

Kamala Harris—15 minutes

Elizabeth Warren—12 minutes

Beto O'Rourke—8 minutes
Pete Buttigieg—7 minutes
Bernie Sanders—7 minutes
Cory Booker—4 minutes
Amy Klobuchar—3 minutes
Julián Castro—1.5 minutes
Andrew Yang—2 seconds

In fact, Andrew's total even puts him behind candidates who *didn't* qualify for the September debate:

Bill de Blasio—2 minutes
Kirsten Gillibrand—59 seconds
Tim Ryan—29 seconds
Tulsi Gabbard—24 seconds
Marianne Williamson—19 seconds
Steve Bullock—12 seconds
John Delaney—12 seconds
John Hickenlooper—11 seconds
Eric Swalwell—10 seconds
Jay Inslee—4 seconds

But it wasn't just the amount of coverage. Here are a few of the more blatant examples of the #YangMediaBlackout.[8]

Omissions from polling graphics:
I've mentioned before that Andrew was often left off cable news graphics. In fact, from the day he qualified for the first debate (March 9, 2019) to the actual debate itself (June 27, 2019), Andrew Yang was omitted from the graphics showing pictures of who was running for president a whopping thirteen times.

But along with being omitted from graphics showing the candidates, he was notably absent from graphics showing poll performance—even once he started polling well! Sometimes it was subtle—the sort of thing most people would never notice, and that could have been dismissed as an honest mistake . . . if it hadn't happened so consistently. They'd show a graphic with two columns, with six name boxes on the left and five on the right, and the empty spot on the right is where

Yang's name would have gone according to the polling, but instead they left him off. Cable news came up with all sorts of weird, off-balance graphics that seemed to go out of their way not to include him.

Other times it was not subtle at all. For instance, when we got 3 percent in a poll and Beto O'Rourke got 1 percent in the same poll, CNN created a graphic displaying the poll results that included Beto and left Andrew off:

This was by no means an isolated incident.

Leaving Andrew off lists in general:
When we raised $10 million in the third quarter of 2019, the fifth-highest fundraising total, CNN left Andrew off their fundraising graphic and instead included Cory Booker—who only raised $6 million. MSNBC did the same thing when reporting cash-on-hand numbers, excluding our campaign's $6.4 million on hand, and including candidates with far less.

When Andrew qualified for the November MSNBC debate, he was consistently omitted from the list of ten candidates who'd done so. "Here are the ten candidates!" the anchor would say, but there were only nine names on the screen—Andrew's, of course, was the only one left off.

And from here it starts to get strange . . .

Calling Andrew the wrong name, using the wrong picture, and other weirdness:

When Andrew crowd-surfed at an event—the sort of quirky thing that was, as we'll discuss soon, the only way we got covered—MSNBC actually referred to him as "John Yang" on-air. "JOHN YANG CROWD SURFS ON 2020 TRAIL" the chyron read across the bottom of the screen, below a shot of Andrew being held aloft by his supporters. (The hashtag #WhoIsJohnYang went briefly viral as a result.)

Another time, CNBC used a picture of a guy named Geoff Yang on their fundraising graphic instead of Andrew.

"Ummm. This is @geoff_yang and I am NOT running for president," the (not Andrew) Yang pictured posted on Twitter, above a screenshot.*

In a particularly odd example from back in July, when MSNBC had Andrew on the air, they displayed the following illustration of his "platform":

Yep . . . those were *definitely* the policy proposals most closely associated with Andrew Yang's campaign.

Finally, as I mentioned in an earlier chapter, Andrew Yang was often characterized as "a billionaire." An MSNBC chyron, for example, referred to him as

---

* https://twitter.com/geoff_yang/status/1214244103174512644?s=20

"billionaire Andrew Yang"—despite the fact that only two other candidates (Buttigieg and Gabbard) had a *lower* net worth than Andrew.

—————

A few weeks after the Des Moines speech, my iPhone was on speaker as I paced around in gym shorts and a bright-blue "I heart Iowa" T-shirt someone had given me on the campaign trail. I was in my New York City sh-itchen,* having just returned from Atlanta, where MSNBC had hosted the last debate, and I was screaming "Don't bullshit a bullshitter!" at the person on the other end of the line—a senior booker for MSNBC.

"You still haven't answered my question," I continued, trying to calm down. "I want to understand. Your network has consistently left Yang off graphics, mentions him less than any other candidate despite the fact that he's currently polling in fifth place—and *rising*—and you didn't ask him a single question for the first thirty-two minutes of the debate! So my question is: If you were in our shoes, how could you possibly see this as anything but a systematic effort by your network to dismiss Andrew Yang? Help me understand."

It was the end of November, and two of our three cars (if you're still tracking my analogies from chapter two) were humming. Fundraising was great—we were on pace to have our best quarter yet. Crowd sizes were fantastic—our rallies drew thousands in every big city in the country. However, our press car had ground to a halt, and it was hurting us greatly.

After our post-Houston breakout in late September, we'd finally gotten mainstream media to pay attention, covering our fundraising success and our giveaway strategy, and we'd allowed ourselves to believe that the "Yang media blackout" was over, or at least would be soon. Andrew was undeniably a contender now; we were leveling up, and surely the coverage of our campaign would level up accordingly. We poured everything into refocusing and repositioning for the next phase of the campaign, kicked off by Andrew's kick-ass speech in Iowa, and the result was . . . total radio silence.

—————

* "Sh-itchen" is not a typo. My studio was an example of a classic Manhattan real estate oddity, in which the shower is located in the kitchen: shower + kitchen = sh-itchen. It didn't bother me; I was a single guy living alone, I loved the neighborhood, and I could cook bacon for breakfast while I showered in the morning.

Sure, we could still get occasional "interesting anomaly" coverage if we did something offbeat, like crowd-surfing or the "Cupid Shuffle." But whenever we did more "traditional" presidential candidate activities—town halls, rallies, even speeches at key Democratic political events—we got *nothing*. Here we were, trying to demonstrate the seriousness of our ideas and the substance of our candidate, but despite polling and fundraising "proving" we deserved it, we couldn't get the kind of basic coverage that all other serious presidential candidates get.

You're so used to seeing it, you probably don't even notice, but serious presidential candidates get:

- Regular coverage of their campaign activities
- Cable news pundits and panelists mentioning their names when discussing politics
- Occasional live or recap coverage of their events/rallies
- Political opinion writers and serious political journalists writing about their messages, policies, and appeal and
- Inclusion in pre-debate coverage, and postdebate coverage of what they said on the stage

We got virtually none of that. We had the grassroots support, the fundraising, the polling numbers and favorables to compete with the other candidates—hell, we even went deeper on policy than plenty of the competition. It didn't matter. We'd leveled up, and as soon as we did, our coverage was dialed back down.

When Andrew first started running, we got the same reaction over and over again: *the DNC will never let you win.*

I saw this thousands of times on Twitter, Instagram, and Reddit, and I heard it in person too. But in fact, the DNC was generally pretty positive toward our campaign—depending upon how you looked at it, they could even be seen as helping us. For example, they could have set the debate participation thresholds higher (as they did in years past). Instead, debate participation began with a polling threshold of only 1 percent—or 65,000 individual donors (rather than a large, total-based funding threshold). That lower polling requirement and grassroots donation path are both supportive of outsider candidates like Andrew Yang. Seema Nanda, who was the executive director of the DNC at the time, is someone Andrew and I consider a friend, and she was always lovely to both of us. In fact, her kids are Yang Gang (I gave her a signed MATH hat for one of them, *shhh*). Even the heads of the state parties—Ray Buckley in New Hampshire and Troy Price in Iowa—were welcoming to our campaign.

No, "the DNC will never let you win" concern was a bit misplaced.

Ultimately, the gatekeeper slamming the door on an Andrew Yang rise was the mainstream media.

Let's pump the brakes and talk about Bud Light for a minute. (Yes, the beer. I promise this is relevant.)

Why does Bud Light advertise? Is it because no one knows what Bud Light is? Is it because they have a new recipe, or a new design or logo to unveil?

Generally, no. Everyone knows Bud Light exists, and everyone knows where to find it. Yet Bud Light spends millions of dollars a year on advertising—commercials, billboards, online, print. Why?

Bud Light generally advertises to normalize their product. So you can go into any bar, anywhere in the country, and order a Bud Light, and no one will blink. So if you're at a party and someone offers you a can of Bud Light, you don't think twice about taking it.

When it comes to politics, mainstream media serves essentially the same function as Bud Light marketing. We trust that Biden or Klobuchar or Harris is a real candidate with a real shot at winning because the mainstream media covers them constantly in the context of the election. All day, every day we read their names, we see their faces, we hear them talked about by experts, and so on. Voting for them is normal and safe. *They* are normal. *They* are safe. They are the political version of Bud Light.

If the traditional candidates who get traditional coverage are Bud Light, Andrew Yang is Sweetwater Brewing Company 420 Extra Pale Ale—a great beer that no one has really heard of. If you like the taste of beer, Sweetwater tastes better. It looks better; it has a cool bottle and a cool story. It's likely more environmentally friendly and supports a local business instead of an international conglomerate. Heck, it has more alcohol in it so it will even get you drunker, if that is your goal. But these direct comparisons don't matter. Sweetwater could be better (and likely is better) than Bud Light in every single category. Regardless, millions of people will still pick Bud Light over Sweetwater when given the choice.

Bud Light is literally created to taste like water—as bland and flavorless as possible. Why would any rational human being pick Bud Light over Sweetwater? Lots of reasons, but most of them boil down to risk. Buying beer for a party and not sure what people will like? Bud Light may be bland, but bland is inoffensive. Ordering a beer at a bar? Why spend extra to try something you have never heard of and may hate? Bud Light is the safer bet. Of course, a number of people still choose Sweetwater (God bless you, independent thinkers and beer connoisseurs). But on average, more people will choose Bud Light.

Now, the risk involved in choosing who to vote for in a national election is way, *way* higher than that involved in maybe spending seven dollars on a beer you don't like. Most people don't enjoy "throwing away" their vote. They want to vote for someone who could win, who is a "serious candidate," and if they're talking politics to their friends, they want to appear well-informed and/or smart by supporting the "right" candidate. Thus, people overwhelmingly choose a candidate who has been normalized (i.e., given the Bud Light treatment) by the media.

Donald Trump is a strong example here. The media loved to hate on Donald Trump. It is estimated that he received $5 *billion* in free media over the course of his 2016 campaign, $2 billion in the primary alone, more than Hillary Clinton, Bernie Sanders, Ted Cruz, Paul Ryan, and Marco Rubio *combined*.[9] And with that volume of coverage—of his campaign, of him in a political context, even though it was negative—he eventually became normalized. And in fact, since his brand was that he was going to blow up our political system, and statistically speaking Republicans don't trust the media, the press attacking him was actually *helpful*.[10]

Bud Light's strategy is all about volume. Because at a certain point, the constant in-your-face marketing of a product makes it tolerable, normal, popular, and safe. Trump, while radical and polarizing in so many ways, was normalized and popularized thanks to political media shivving him 24-7. If you don't like the other choices, and all you see is Trump Trump Trump everywhere, you start thinking he might be a real option for president. And *that's* why who and what the media chooses to cover makes or breaks campaigns.

Despite owning the alternative media space and competing well in the attention economy, in order to win an election with more than 150 million people voting, and specifically to win a Democratic primary, in which 73 percent of voters trust (and rely upon the judgment of) mass media, the Andrew Yang campaign needed a little bit more help from the national mainstream political media to reach the next level.[11] And we never got it. The media's response to Andrew Yang's rise in popularity as a 2020 presidential candidate was not to cover him like the upstart in fifth place and moving up, and it wasn't to start covering him like any other candidate, and it wasn't to ridicule him either. Nope. It was far, far worse. It was to ignore him.

Which brings me back to what had me screaming at the MSNBC booker: the final straw—the November 2019 debate, hosted by MSNBC. During which Andrew Yang was not asked a single question for the first thirty-two minutes of the debate.

We expected, based on our experience so far, that MSNBC wasn't going to be friendly toward Andrew that night. So we prepped extra hard, wanting to be ready for whatever they threw at us. We figured they would hit Andrew with aggressive questions, deliberately mischaracterize his stances, or throw "gotcha" nonsense his way, but never did we anticipate that they would straight-up ignore him. Maybe that was on us, but we all believed (our new expert political consultants included) that it was essentially part of the unwritten journalistic rules that, if someone gets on the debate stage, they at least get the proportionate number of questions based on their poll position.

Now, Andrew wasn't a front-runner, so we didn't expect to dominate the time, but, for context, Elizabeth Warren, who was polling just two spots ahead of us, was asked five questions during those opening thirty-two minutes. Every single other candidate was asked at least one question during this window. Even Cory Booker, who was polling last out of all the candidates onstage, was asked a direct question during this window and brought into multiple back-and-forths. As the candidate polling fifth in a field of ten, we reasonably expected Andrew would get at least two questions in the opening half hour.

But nope. No questions for thirty-two minutes. Importantly, that was two minutes *after* the thirty-minute mark, the exact time when the number of viewers of a prime-time event starts to decline.[12] Andrew Yang finished the debate dead last in speaking time, with a total of six minutes and forty-three seconds.[13] For comparison, Cory Booker spoke for nearly twelve minutes, Kamala Harris spoke for just over eleven minutes, and Amy Klobuchar spoke for just under eleven minutes—and all three of these candidates were polling lower than Andrew.[14]

If you considered yourself a Yang Gang member and you're reading this now, you likely remember screaming at the TV at various moments during the campaign, "WHY AREN'T YOU COVERING ANDREW YANG!?" I can assure you that our entire team was right there with you the whole time. But by November, when I was doing my screaming into the phone in my sh-itchen, the lack of coverage was no longer just frustrating or even infuriating—it was an existential threat, torpedoing our hard-won momentum and making it impossible to reach the next level.

The first question we asked ourselves, of course, was: *Why are they ignoring us?*

If "follow the money" is your first thought . . . we were great from a bottom-line standpoint: Andrew's appearances got some of the highest ratings and social media engagement rates of all the candidates. We had an *amazing* story: a nontraditional candidate with an inexperienced team had come out of nowhere to crack the top five in a crowded field of Democratic heavy hitters! By any measure, the Yang campaign should have been one of the biggest stories of the election cycle. Maybe, you're thinking, Andrew Yang was a bad interview subject or secretly an asshole and no one wanted to work with him—but the opposite appeared to be true. Seemingly *everyone* liked him on a personal level, from reporters and anchors to producers to sound guys, and he was smart, funny, and articulate. CNN even gave him a job after he dropped out of the race.

Early in the race, it was at least plausible that our lack of coverage was due to a perception of first irrelevance and then "unseriousness." Much as we wanted to be included in early lists of candidates, for a long time no one had any reason to expect that our campaign was going anywhere. And given the criticism the media got for covering and legitimizing Trump in 2016, they might have been understandably anxious to be seen as caring more about political bona fides than political theater, making them more likely to cover *any* elected official (even one we were outpolling) than "the free money guy." This had been our working assumption, and why we expected things to turn around that fall. By then, we were in the top five, indisputably no longer irrelevant, and we'd changed up our strategy to broaden Andrew's support among voters by emphasizing his depth and humanity.

So why were we getting less coverage than ever?

Any time I talked to producers and reporters about it, they'd tell me that Andrew needed to do more things "worth covering." Sadly, what is "worth covering" is determined by the media companies themselves, and what was worth covering for *other* candidates somehow wasn't for us. Andrew Yang had some of the biggest rallies in the field, and not a single one was ever streamed live (including, eventually, his concession speech—something that is almost always covered for major candidates). Somehow, anything we did that was "serious" was not "worth covering."

We may never know all the details of what was behind the #YangMediaBlackout in general. I have plenty of thoughts, but what's most relevant (and applicable far beyond politics) is something more specific, namely why that blackout got suddenly so much blacker as we tried to level up. We may never know all the details of that for sure, either, but I can make a pretty educated deduction that a big part of it was that a leveled-up Andrew Yang did not fit the media's narrative for him. We weren't ever going to get "serious candidate" coverage because that wasn't the role they had cast us in, and no polling or fundraising numbers were going to change that. If we wanted to act the part of gimmick candidate, they might (*might*) cover it, but anything that didn't "fit," they'd simply ignore.

Which brings us to the second question we had to ask ourselves, namely: *What do we do about it?*

We needed the press to cover us. Much as we might have wanted to, we couldn't just say "screw them!" and move on. We knew we needed to level up to win, but we also knew that no coverage was worse than the wrong coverage. You play the cards you're dealt, even if you know it's not a winning hand.

And thus we went to work, dedicating resources to things we knew would force the political press to at least mention Andrew's name.

Timely nonpolitical endorsements:
We got endorsements from the most popular nonpolitical people we could, including Elon Musk, Donald Glover, and Dave Chappelle. Donald Glover endorsed us the day before the December debate, and (predictably) Andrew received more coverage for this than for the debate itself. We dropped news of the Dave Chappelle endorsement the day before the January debate to distract from the fact that we hadn't qualified (we weren't polling high enough). We got more coverage for that endorsement than most candidates did for their performance at the debate the next night, and this actually bumped us up in the polls enough to qualify for the final debate in New Hampshire.

War with the press:
Our campaign hadn't really complained publicly about the media coverage situation. Andrew and I both understood that media companies, even those that focus on news, are ultimately entertainment companies, and they can cover what they want—complaining about this wasn't going to solve anything. But, at a certain point, we had to call it out, and that point was when there seemed to be active efforts at MSNBC to erase Andrew Yang. I watched anchor Chris Matthews scream "WHY WOULD YOU DO THAT!?" at his staffer for booking us on his show after one of the debates. Senior producer Ariana Pekary eventually told us on our podcast that she was instructed not to cover Andrew Yang while she worked at MSNBC.

Shortly after being ignored on their debate stage, Andrew made a public statement announcing that he would not appear on any MSNBC program until they apologized on air. There is nothing the media loves covering more than themselves, so this got covered by everyone (except our BFFs at MSNBC). It also rallied our supporters and even helped us raise a decent amount of money as a result.

Yang gone wild:
We tried to give the press what they wanted while still moving forward with our leveled-up strategy. In practice, this meant putting Andrew in authentic situations where he could go viral. In other words, we continued showcasing a more thoughtful, human side of Andrew Yang, while also looking for ways to engage with the public that would appeal to the press. We rationalized this as not being a return to gimmicky campaigning because all candidates do things like this to seem relatable and get attention. (How many times have you seen serious candidates dancing awkwardly at some high school pep rally they showed up at as a "surprise," or "dropping by" a local restaurant/Little League game to do something that makes a good photo op?) Andrew did the "Cupid Shuffle" dance at a Jazzercise class, showed up at random rock concerts, and as mentioned before, even crowd-surfed at an event (which was effective, but frankly a bit dangerous).

It sucked, because we knew that none of the press coverage we managed to create this way was the kind we needed to win the election, but becoming irrelevant was worse for everyone—not just the campaign, but the movement as a whole. Unfortunately, even with our leveled-up team and candidate using every ounce of energy, we had to think outside of the box—we were fighting an impossible battle.

––––––––

I know what you're thinking.

Cry me a river, Zach. The media didn't cover your candidate. Tough cookies, kid. You made this bed with your marketing gimmicks. If you were a better campaign manager, you would've overcome it—or avoided this situation in the first place.

And maybe you're right. I dove into the details of the #YangMediaBlackout and rattled off all these examples because I wanted to give you context and let you see how we experienced this in real time. But the point isn't that the media is messed up or that we got screwed at times; it's that there is something to learn from this chapter in our campaign's evolution—our own mistakes very much included— that is valuable to anyone trying to build a movement and a brand from nothing.

The lesson here, in the end, isn't about political media, or even media at all, it is something much more fundamental:

What got you here won't get you there.

The powerful identity brand we had worked so hard to create was working against us. It had been perfect for an outsider trying to break into the field and stand out in the attention economy, but it didn't quite fit where we wanted to end up. This wasn't a complete surprise to us, but we thought we'd be able to shift the way we presented our identity, de-emphasizing some things and emphasizing others as we went from upstart to contender. The problem was that we'd underestimated the resistance we'd face in doing so. Sure, voters' attention spans are shorter and we forget many things fairly quickly, but it is very difficult to undo, evolve, or change a strong identity brand once you've established one. The strengths and tactics we'd cultivated to take Andrew Yang from unknown man to national sensation were not the same ones we needed to take him from national sensation to president of the United States.

Many of the things that had helped fuel Andrew's rise to prominence were either no longer as helpful or sometimes even hurtful once he reached the level of serious contender. In part, this was because the two levels rewarded different qualities, but mostly it was because the audience we were trying to capture was suddenly a million times broader.

	Upside as a Longshot	Downside as a Contender
Podcasts	Provide a new avenue to connect with people in a long-form and authentic way.	Not an effective way to reach the majority of Democratic primary voters.
Memes	A fun, shareable, and on-message tool to grow our support, particularly online.	Not effective at reaching older primary voters who spend less time online, and memes can potentially be seen as unprofessional or inappropriate.
MATH	Provides a rallying cry for supporters, and a way to lean in to Andrew's identity as a math nerd who will bring logic and reason to the White House.	Reinforces impression of Andrew as just a numbers guy rather than as a father with deep, thoughtful reasons behind his run. Not broadly appealing (who actually likes math class?) and can be viewed as playing into racial stereotypes.
Being Funny	Makes Andrew relatable, human, and authentic.	Great for other contenders with less to prove in terms of experience and ability to handle the presidency, but can make Andrew seem unserious about the job.
Status as an Outsider	Attractive to those tired of traditional politicians and looking for new energy, outside perspective, and big ideas to help the country.	Emphasizes Andrew's inexperience, makes him seem like a political lightweight and a risk to vote for.
The Yang Gang	A die-hard base of supporters bringing passion, energy, resources, and legitimacy to our outsider campaign.	Often portrayed as a unique cult of internet trolls who don't normally vote Democratic.
Nontraditional Endorsements	An exciting and legitimizing way to garner press coverage and coolness by association.	Depending on the endorser, can make Andrew seem niche and weird—Elon Musk endorsed us, but he also endorsed Kanye West, so ...
Emphasis on Grassroots Donors	We built a powerful fundraising bloc of passionate supporters, and Andrew didn't have to spend time doing high-dollar fundraisers.	The big bundlers and power players in the Democratic Party (who also influence the press) did not have relationships with Andrew.

It was a catch-22. In order to get to a place where we had *a chance* to win the Democratic primary, we needed to run an out-of-the-box, uniquely branded campaign. However, by running an out-of-the-box, uniquely branded campaign, we disqualified ourselves from *actually winning* the Democratic primary, because while becoming a contender required us to stand out and get noticed as an outsider, winning required us to reassure voters that we were safe, trustworthy, and broadly appealing enough to beat Donald Trump. We needed to be Sweetwater 420 Pale Ale AND Bud Light, but the Sweetwater-type things we did to make Andrew Yang relevant ensured he'd never achieve Bud Light status—which made him unelectable in this race.*

Regardless, in the end, Andrew was one of the most liked candidates in the field, and he was most people's second or third pick for president. But he was not safe enough to be their top choice, i.e., the person they actually voted for.[15]

As we transitioned from longshot to contender, our newly hired consultants insisted that Andrew needed to be more traditional to win, but the nonpolitical senior leaders who had been with Andrew from the start thought this eliminated our greatest strength and made us play a game we couldn't win. They were both right.

Okay, Zach, now that you know this, how do you solve it? How DO you level up a powerful identity brand that is about shaking up the status quo into a brand that is palatable to the masses?

Well for starters, the climate matters a lot—the industry, the time, general public feeling. Some of these things are beyond your control, and while you can (and should) take them into account, they can also change unpredictably. I'll talk about this in more detail in the book's final chapter.

But leveling up from a niche brand that is disrupting what is mainstream to a brand that is widely popular enough to be the new mainstream—without changing your brand entirely and becoming inauthentic—is very possible. Again, Apple is a perfect example. But it isn't easy, and it is especially hard to do in politics, and even harder to do in a short time frame. The best strategy to combat this, in

---

* *But wait, Zach, how come Trump didn't have this problem?* This is a loaded question, but quickly: (1) Trump was already at 99 percent name recognition—he was normalized for decades by appearing on television in *The Apprentice*, commercials, and even movies; (2) Republicans are different—as mentioned before, they trust media less, so getting hammered in the press helped Trump in ways it wouldn't help a Democrat; (3) The Republican traditional gatekeepers started to line up behind Trump more than any traditional gatekeepers ever lined up behind Andrew.

theory, is the Goldilocks strategy. In our case, this would have meant striking a perfect balance between outsider and established politico. We'd want just enough outsider fun-loving energy, and just enough insider and establishment buy in, to create a candidate who was just right. Or, as we used to discuss in our leadership meetings, the perfect Andrew Yang is somewhere between him breaking down in tears while consoling the mother of a four-year-old who was killed by gun violence at a national forum (a real thing that happened), and him spraying whipped cream in supporters' mouths át a campaign event in New Hampshire (also a real thing that happened). Human and authentic, but not so human you're seen as too emotional for the job, and not so authentic that you seem unserious or weird.

(Ugh, it makes me sick just to type that. Politics is soulless.)

We did try to achieve this balance, especially at first. After all, we began by showcasing a candidate who was both serious and new, who could move between the worlds of long-form podcasts and internet memes . . . but in our desperation to stay relevant, we started spending too much time at one end of that spectrum. In hindsight, I should have prioritized playing the traditional game sooner. Our whole team was caught up in blowing up the system along the lines of what I showed you earlier in this book: *The game has changed. The traditional gatekeepers of power are cracking. We are the future.*

These statements are still true—but as I've warned again and again, they're not absolute. So the best move would have been to plan for that Goldilocks strategy early on, and find a way to maintain that balanced perspective and positioning.

In our case, practically speaking, while our inexperienced, entrepreneurial team was an asset early in the campaign, more experience and connections could have helped us as we tried to compete at a higher level—specifically, a more connected communications staff might have had a better chance of overcoming the media roadblocks we faced. In a perfect world, maybe we would've hit the political networking trail hard after Andrew's performance in July at the Detroit debate. Pre-Detroit, experienced political consultants wouldn't have taken our calls, but after his performance at that debate, we absolutely would have had a few intrigued enough to take a meeting. We could have made the rounds of the DC circuit, connecting with senior staffers, surrogates, endorsers, and high-dollar donors connected to the candidates who were dropping in the polls while we were rising. I could have spent August laying the groundwork to build an experienced political team: *Hey, I know you're with so-and-so candidate, but watch out for Andrew Yang this fall, he's poised for a breakout.* And then I would have been ready to pull the trigger on hiring after Andrew's September debate giveaway went viral (and we had the cash).

This would have set us up with a seasoned communications team in the door by mid-September, which would have let us put together a compelling national communications plan to break through as a serious contender after our $10 million fundraising haul at the end of the third quarter. We could have hyped our leveled-up strategy to reporters—who might have been more likely to take seriously communications professionals they already knew—for all of October, culminating in Andrew's speech at the Liberty and Justice Celebration in November, and maybe had more luck in becoming a story (or *the* story) that night, instead of just a line in a CNN wrap-up.

That might have led to more friendly and serious press treatment in general, and heck, even some better questions from MSNBC at the November debate, and a resulting polling bump around Thanksgiving that could have catapulted us into the top tier with just two months to go before the Iowa caucuses.

Of course, this all sounds good, and there's even a chance it would have worked . . . And there's also a chance that the best political professionals in the world would've come into the campaign and still failed to move the media and change the narratives. Plus, this would have been a bigger gamble than it sounds like, because we had no clue that we would raise $10 million in grassroots funding in the third quarter (much of it came the last few weeks). So even if we'd planned to go Goldilocks earlier, we might not have been able to execute the right Goldilocks strategy for our situation—not without the knowledge that we only acquired once it was over.

The discouraging fact is that *what got you here won't always get you there* is both absolutely true but not always possible to plan for. (Making sure your brand fits the moment is something we'll discuss in the final chapter.) The best advice I can give is this:

Make sure that your identity brand fits where you ultimately want to end up, not just where you're going next.

But importantly, as frustrating as our inability to level up was, the root of this problem wasn't just about the press (or lack of it), or even the mismatch between our longshot tactics and our contender status. These things were all symptoms of maybe the most fundamental challenge of our whole campaign: the fact that we were building our plane while flying it.

8

DEFINE YOUR COLLECTIVE SUCCESS

Building the Plane While Flying

We need to seriously talk about dropping out if we don't perform well in New Hampshire.

—**Me**

WE WERE THREE DAYS REMOVED FROM A DISAPPOINTING IOWA CAUCUS NIGHT, AND once again, I found myself across from Andrew, facing a conversation that neither of us wanted to have. It was late morning, and the sun was reflecting off the snow-covered sidewalks of Manchester, New Hampshire, and into the room at the Holiday Inn Express that we had booked for debate prep. Andrew was slouched in the corner, grateful not to be in front of a crowd for the moment, and our gathered team mirrored his exhausted energy.

Iowa had been a double disappointment. The inability of the Iowa Democratic Party to reliably count the ballots meant the results were in disarray, which was disappointing from a general "faith in our democracy" standpoint. But as much as we wanted to complain about the ineptitude of certain political professionals (*you had ONE job!*), their incompetence had essentially zero effect on our campaign. Which brings me to the second, larger disappointment: our performance. The dust had settled enough to see that we'd received just over 5 percent of the popular vote and 1 percent of the state delegate equivalents, finishing in sixth place. And not a close sixth place, a very distant sixth place—the fifth-place finisher, Amy Klobuchar, had gotten 12.7 percent of the popular vote and a similar percentage of delegates—so despite our most optimistic beliefs that they counted our votes wrong, too, no recount was actually going to save us.

Naturally, spirits were pretty low, and there were now just five days before the New Hampshire primary.

"We've discussed," I said to Andrew, motioning to a few senior leaders who had joined us in the hotel room, "and we think your best bet, if we don't do well here in New Hampshire on election night, is for you to take that opportunity to bow out of the race with your head held high."

Andrew stayed slouched in silence as he took this in.

With the beginning of primary voting in Iowa three days before, it felt like we had just completed the longest and most exhausting roller coaster of our lives.

Actually, "exhausting" doesn't really do it justice. Neither does the roller coaster analogy.

More accurately, we were one step from dead. Shells of human beings. Nothing can prepare you for the reality of a presidential campaign, let alone a longshot, upstart, built-on-the-fly presidential campaign like ours. David Axelrod (Obama's chief campaign strategist) called presidential campaigns "MRIs for the soul";[1] I would compare *our* run to the Zipper ride at a cheap carnival. In the carnival version, you sit strapped in a cage that rockets straight up and plummets back down again while also flipping and spinning in unpredictable directions. As soon as you feel like you're in control and the spinning has stopped, you'll find yourself upside down again, spinning in some new way you didn't know was possible. Our presidential campaign was that Zipper ride—but muuuuuuch longer. At the end of both, you emerge dizzy, a little nauseous, and not entirely sure of who you are or how you got there.

To be fair, it's not all bad, not by a longshot (ha). The people are amazing—so committed and passionate, they restored my faith in humanity whenever it started to take a beating. One field organizer we met had slipped on some black ice while canvassing and broke his leg . . . he went out canvassing the next day on crutches. Some of my favorite moments were bonding with the team on the bus or in a small-town bar, exhausted but sharing the misery, mission, and, frankly, mystery: *Are our efforts making a difference? We won't know 'til caucus night.* And despite our problems with the press in general, we all had a lot of fun hanging out with the reporters off the record, and I think they genuinely liked us, too—our crew of misfits had to be an interesting change from the seasoned politico types they normally encountered. There is also a certain beauty to seeing our democracy in action, imperfect as it is. I could go on, but you get the idea. The Yang campaign was a once-in-a-lifetime experience, and the day-to-day was exhilarating. Plus, campaign buses are pretty sweet.

But the closer we got to the Iowa caucuses, the more draining it got.

Whether or not they personally liked us, the press wasn't giving us much coverage, so with a few weeks to go before the first votes were cast, we'd decided to barnstorm as much of Iowa as possible to speak to voters directly. This generally sucks and is one of the most exhausting and lowest return-on-investment strategies in all of politics. But as it was our only real option, we begrudgingly embraced the suck of retail politics in Iowa winter.

Andrew did four to seven in-person events per day, for seventeen days straight—and each event was at least a ninety-minute drive from every other, so we were typically on the road by 6 AM and didn't return to the hotel until close to midnight. It was relentless and intense, especially since these events had an average crowd size of only one hundred people or so (not bad for rural Iowa), which meant it wasn't like swooping in for some big keynote speech and sneaking out the back, it was constant engagement with potential voters.

The time on the road sucked because it meant trying to run the campaign over bad cell service or spotty Wi-Fi. The food sucked because there was no time for anything but greasy fast food scarfed down on the go. The weather sucked because it was a bone-chilling negative ten degrees with Midwest winds blowing it in your face. The hotels sucked because they were whatever we could find in the middle of whatever Iowa town we were in. The luggage situation sucked because you were going to be gone for seventeen days but had to fit everything in a carry-on bag to maximize bus space (and avoid baggage fees for the plane ride *to* Iowa), meaning your bag was so stuffed you had to unpack everything every day to find anything, and you still needed to do laundry about ten days in. The sleep schedule sucked because we were leaving early and getting back late, and never staying in the same place twice meant getting up even earlier to repack your bag and make sure you hadn't forgotten your charger/toothbrush/etc.—which you inevitably would at some point, making the next day suck even more.

Andrew, who, again, had gone a *decade* without a sick day, was so drained by our whirlwind tour of Iowa that he got ungodly ill for the second time in less than a year. This time, it lasted a week. For seven very long days, he had a nasty cough and his voice was barely audible. His eyes were so itchy and swollen he couldn't put his contacts in, and we were subjected to his nerd jokes that he was doing his events "Daredevil style!"—as in the Marvel superhero who is blind but still manages to beat up the bad guys. Occasional joke aside, every event that week seemed to take all of Andrew's strength just to get through; as soon as it was over, he retreated to the bus, flipped off his shoes, put his jacket over his head, and slept until we arrived at our next stop.

But to be frank, as we approached the Iowa primary, the real reason that campaigning felt even more like a Zipper ride from hell than usual isn't because Andrew got sick or because we were confined to a bus or because Iowa in winter is a frozen hellscape. No, it boils down to the cumulative mental exhaustion of not just building a presidential campaign from nothing but growing it on the fly at breakneck speed. The pace of our growth had leapt at several points in the race, but none as dramatic as what we experienced after the September debate. For context, between September 2019 and January 2020 alone:[2]

- We went from a few hundred thousand to nearly three million social media followers
- Our email list grew from about 100,000 to nearly one million subscribers
- The number of individual donors to the Yang campaign grew from 130,000 to nearly 450,000
- Yang Gang volunteer chapters expanded from a few thousand volunteers in major cities to tens of thousands of volunteers with chapters in every single state nationwide
- We opened dozens of new campaign offices across Iowa and New Hampshire
- Our presence in the early primary states of Nevada and South Carolina grew from one or two staffers each to over thirty full-time employees across each state
- We built ballot access operations from scratch in almost all fifty states, collecting tens of thousands of signatures to make sure we got Andrew Yang's name on each state's primary election ballot

- Our NYC HQ expanded from one small office to take over the entire floor of our midtown office building and
- We raised $23.2 million—more than double what we had raised in the nearly two years since we entered the race

And my favorite stat:

- We hired over three hundred full-time employees in the span of just a few months, taking us from a small team of just forty people working full-time to a large-scale national operation

Now of course, like any good campaign, we shouted from the mountaintops about every achievement, trumpeting every morsel of positive momentum to the world. So from the outside looking in, we were on fire. But the truth is, this type of growth was not fun. It was chaos.

Frankly, building *anything* at this scale, this fast, will be a hot mess no matter what. But some sudden take-off situations are definitely easier than others. For instance, if your start-up business was rapidly growing and got a quick investment of $10 million, you could take some time to decide how best to deploy that money based on your needs and goals—heck, realistically you've already mapped out spending and hiring plans, identified needs in terms of talent, infrastructure, and IT spends, and strategized marketing campaigns in order to even receive that investment. As a different example, if you're a small handcrafted jewelry shop and a major celebrity or influencer decides to buy one of your necklaces and post about it on Instagram, you'll receive a crazy number of orders and visits to your website. But in the wake of the blowup, you don't have to do everything at once—you can keep filling orders, communicate about the supply delays, and scale and hire thoughtfully. Similarly, if you are a band that receives a ton of newfound fame, you can announce a tour date in a few weeks or months and take your time to improve operations and processes.

In our case, the Andrew Yang campaign's most massive influx of money, people, and national attention not only happened unexpectedly and overnight, it also required an immediate response. There was no time to stop, step back, and thoughtfully scale up—we were in the middle of a campaign! We needed a bigger and more professionalized operation to reflect our newfound status in the race, AND we needed to continue running the operations we already had. In other words, *we had to build the plane while it was flying.* Not a single department was able to strategically plan ahead—how could they!? We'd spent the majority of the campaign just trying to survive. The message before September was *Do what you can with what you have (which isn't much)*, and the message after September was *Build a national organization to compete with the top contenders (and do it yesterday)*.

Even if you have a "what if I go viral" contingency plan, the mechanics of scaling up that quickly are brutal . . . and bordering on impossible. Now, don't get me wrong: I'm *thrilled* we had our breakout. I'm incredibly grateful that we grew so fast that our problems became about scaling, and not just convincing people to care like in previous months. That said, I also want to emphasize that if you are fortunate enough to be in a similar situation—trying to build a (much bigger) plane while keeping your existing aircraft at cruising altitude—I can say with 100 percent confidence that every single process you have will break.

Take hiring (and firing). When I worked on Wall Street, the process of filling five open positions would take nine months to a year; on our campaign, sometimes a department had to hire five people in *one day*. Have an employee onboarding process that worked for thirty people? Awesome. Try it for one hundred people. Then double that. Oh, and some of those people are in Iowa or New Hampshire or South Carolina, which follow different labor laws than your headquarters in New York City. In our case, plenty of people came from out of state to work on the campaign without permanently relocating, which meant factoring in their home states as well. It was immensely time consuming, and a burden on our already over-worked staff—none of whom, at the time, were experts in human resources. Hiring logistics and management became a strategic priority for the campaign overnight.

And to top it off, we finally had the cash to staff up field organizers in October and November 2019; positions that the Warren, Biden, Sanders, Buttigieg, O'Rourke, and Harris campaigns were able to fill back in March! With the majority of veteran staffers already committed to more established operations, we were mainly hiring people with lots of ambition but minimal or no political experience. I know, I know, *that basically describes our whole original team*. This is true, but there's a big difference between a handful of inexperienced people working as a tight-knit team in the beginnings of a start-up, and hundreds of inexperienced people scattered around the country as part of a full-scale, quickly evolving national organization. This required more training and investment from the few people we had with experience, which slowed our already behind-the-eight-ball operation even more.

But as hard as hiring on the fly was, firing was worse.

Given the short timeline of a campaign, and the fact that we weren't complete assholes, our goal during this period of rapid growth was to avoid firing anyone unless it was absolutely necessary. Start-ups usually like to hire fast and fire fast, but for us, firing someone was the worst possible outcome: we tried to give people the opportunity to improve, we tried to work around their weaknesses, we tried to move underperformers into other or better-fitting roles, anything we could do to avoid it.

Besides the not-being-assholes part (many of our new hires had literally moved from out of state to work for the campaign), there are a couple of reasons why firing was the worst possible outcome for our campaign. For one thing, it meant using valuable time to find and train someone new . . . again. For another, firing people increased your risk of distracting and off-message stories about the campaign's "culture" or "staff issues." People who are fired are generally not happy about it, and the drama-hungry press was always eager to lend a sympathetic ear. Literally every campaign has experienced this—here are just a few headlines about other Democratic contenders during the 2020 presidential race:

"Bernie Sanders staffers complained about the campaign's use of Amazon, a frequent Sanders target" (*Washington Post*[3])

"Women of color bolt Warren's Nevada campaign in frustration" (*Politico*[4])

"How People of Color Inside the Buttigieg Campaign Sought to Be Heard" (*New York Times*[5])

"Kamala Harris Campaign Accused of Treating Staff 'So Poorly' and Not Having 'a Real Plan to Win'" (*Newsweek*[6])

No campaign escapes staff problems. You combine rapid growth, rushed timelines, young staff, high-stress environments, passionate people, and trigger-happy press watching your every move—it's a recipe for disaster. I'm proud of the campaign we ran and the leaders who put in the thankless work of building a massive national organization on the fly. I'll also be the first to admit we could have been better. Our reluctance to fire people sometimes worked against us: We had bad hires who weren't fired fast enough. We had feedback mechanisms in place to make sure Andrew and I were kept aware of issues at the field offices, but sometimes these broke down, and we learned about personnel problems too late. Worst of all, there were times when I *did* hear about a problem but didn't get complete information, and I made the wrong decision about how to handle it as a result, only to discover later it had been more serious than I'd known or had worsened since.

The fact that campaigns are crazy is not an excuse to brush personnel issues under the rug. It was heartbreaking to find that we hadn't always lived up to our "Humanity First" values; Andrew and I took it personally. But blue-chip corporations with stacked HR departments spend millions of dollars a year on handling staffing issues and building company culture and often still get it wrong. Expecting an organization built on the fly to be better at this is fundamentally ridiculous.

Then again, building a national organization on the fly is a ridiculous exercise, so I guess this comes with the territory. Hiring is only one of many, many examples of the high-stakes areas this kind of rapid scaling will pressure test or upend entirely. *Oh, you have an expense approval process that works for your thirty-person staff?* Surprise! You now have eighty new field staffers in Iowa and another fifty in New Hampshire, and they all need to pay for crap. You now need people and software to manage their spending and make sure you don't give the wrong people credit card access or bankrupt the campaign, and you need it now.

Hiring, expense approval, management, reporting, internal communications, data access, merch inventory and delivery, print materials, canvassing, cybersecurity, donor communications, and more—every single process we had broke in real time and then had to be reevaluated, reinvested in, and rebuilt on the fly. Every day was an exercise in trailblazing, all the while knowing that the organization we were building could die in Iowa right after caucus night—or really at any time at all.

Part of building the plane while flying is retooling it to fit changing conditions; we were constantly, as you've seen throughout this book, making changes to our strategy to adapt to whatever new challenge we faced. Whether it was deciding to focus on getting 65,000 donors or deciding to give away money at the September debate, these decisions happened in the middle of all the everyday chaos of a campaign.

But another part of building your plane while flying is knowing when to stop trying to climb higher—accepting that at some point, attempting to reach new heights risks bringing the whole thing crashing down.

Which brings me back to why I was sitting across from Andrew in the Manchester Holiday Inn Express to talk about dropping out of the race.

On one hand, we had always intended to stick it out to the convention, if at all possible. Andrew had even publicly told supporters that he planned to duke it out until the party picked a nominee. The reasoning behind this was simple: if we could go into the convention with a few delegates, we could give universal basic income a voice at a major political party's convention for the first time and advocate for its adoption in the platform—or at least its wider acceptance.

On the other hand, we needed to look at the big picture. We'd missed the January debate, we hadn't shocked the world in Iowa, and, as we sat in a hotel room in New Hampshire, we weren't feeling fantastic about our chances in that state either. On our gauntlet tour through Iowa, we had done more events in the state than any other candidate in the field, and today (three days after caucus night) was now day 727 of the campaign. We were physically and mentally fried. Andrew and I had just spent two years on the Zipper ride from hell—for a 1 percent finish.

At this point, there was one question we needed to consider:

Why are we doing this?

We knew why we were running. To bring attention to the problems no one was talking about, and the logical solutions that could move our society forward. To save society from the fourth industrial revolution. To wake America up to the threat and reality of automation and the need to rewrite the rules of our economy. To bring universal basic income into the public and political consciousness. To accelerate our society toward a future that we could feel good about leaving for our children.

So while winning the presidency was the ideal outcome, there were many versions of success that did not involve Andrew Yang in the Oval Office. And if President Andrew Yang was not in the cards, we needed to optimize for those. To ensure that our army, and our movement, lived on long beyond this election.

Which brings us to the last strategy in our playbook, and the very best way to combat the challenges of building the plane while flying:

Define your collective success.

Whatever arena you're competing in will have its own definition of success—generally speaking, most of us are market driven, so success will be defined by some combination of money, power, and/or fame for your identity brand.

These things are not inherently wrong to strive for, of course. But that striving should be driven by the "like us" identity that you collectively share with your supporters. If it isn't, it can ruin what you've built.

Let's revisit the jewelry example from earlier. Say you've built a strong identity brand around your handcrafted, high-quality necklaces, selling them on Etsy and working to get them carried by a few local boutiques. Then Taylor Swift buys one, posts about it on Instagram, and your brand becomes a global fashion trend overnight. The plane you're flying is going to need some upgrades—fast. But *what* upgrades you make should depend upon how you have defined your collective success with your supporters. If your initial tribe has come along for the ride because they think you are building the next Tiffany & Co.—then by all means, go for it. Get investors, scale operations, and become an international conglomerate off your newfound fame. However, if your initial tribe was all about "handmade" jewelry crafted by a small local business, then perhaps you will collectively define success a bit differently. In this case, maybe the best way to upgrade your plane is to hire other artisans so that all pieces continue to be handmade at scale. Or maybe you simply increase the price of the jewelry you create, making the brand more exclusive but also rewarding your initial supporters (who now own something more valuable).

There is no "right" answer, but there are definitely wrong answers here. Identity branding is all about letting people personally identify with you, so the key is to define your success collectively, with them in mind. You've spent all this time and energy letting them become a part of your brand—*there's no real success that doesn't include them!* A strong identity brand has a sharp sense of exactly who their supporters are, listens to them, and is able to make important strategic decisions that remain true to why supporters felt a "like us" connection in the first place.

In our case, Andrew hadn't started this campaign just because he wanted to be president, and no one on the team had joined because they thought it was a sure path to a cushy job at the White House. We were all on this metaphorical plane together because we believed we were a part of something that mattered, something more than a campaign.

And that was the big picture to focus on.

Collective success for us wasn't solely about the presidential race. You could argue that it never had been.

Our collective success was always about the movement.

And if we looked at our options in terms of our collective success, outside of just winning and losing the election, staying in any longer would be the wrong move.

This was hard to swallow. We were all die-hard supporters who truly believed we were working to elect the next president of the United States! But if we lost badly in New Hampshire as expected, and Andrew decided to stay in the race anyway, we wouldn't just be facing irrelevance (our worst enemy)—all of our work to build this remarkable brand and movement was at risk of being completely undone.

The right move was to make the decision about when and how to drop out by focusing on what was best for our movement. If we wanted these ideas to outlast our campaign, we needed to retool the plane with that future in mind.

This is what I outlined for Andrew sitting in the Manchester Holiday Inn Express.

"We either exit gracefully after the New Hampshire primary," I said, "or don't drop out, and continue on a death march through Nevada, South Carolina, and Super Tuesday. Every stop will yield smaller crowds, potential embarrassment and ridicule, and the fundraising will dry up, so we'll be working with less and less. If you think the press has ignored us so far, this will be substantially worse. I think timing your dropout effectively is the best way to keep this movement growing beyond this election."

Andrew did not like this plan, and he was vocal about it. "I don't give a shit about being embarrassed. I started this campaign when no one cared, and I'm happy to end it when no one cares. We're running to bring awareness to the fourth industrial revolution. To promote universal basic income, and convince our elected officials to humanize our economy. We're not running for my ego."

"I know," I replied. "But looking at the numbers, I think that if you don't help the party line up behind one candidate to beat Donald, and keep fighting for attention on your own campaign, there's a real chance that the favorability you worked so hard to grow for this movement will take a significant hit."

Someone else jumped in, and for a while the team in the room went back and forth with Andrew, talking polling and probabilities until finally I cut back in, silencing the debate to level with him as a friend.

"All right. This isn't the experts talking. This isn't even Campaign Manager Zach talking. This is the friend you sat with in that coffee shop three years ago, and I'm talking to you, Andrew, the man, not the candidate."

I paused.

"I'll follow you wherever you want to take this thing. But I'd encourage you to think big picture. If we don't win this election, we can still look ourselves in the eye and say *MISSION ACCOMPLISHED*. We've put universal basic income on the map! It's never had more support and momentum, and that is because of what we've built.

"We're at a point now where if you stay in the race when you're no longer a serious candidate for president, there's a solid chance we'll destroy what we just worked so hard to build. If you start putting up one percent or worse on election night in Nevada, South Carolina, and beyond, our movement is going to look like a fringe idea all over again. We've fought hard to legitimize your ideas, and we finally have. If dropping out with grace keeps universal basic income in a positive light . . . it's hard, but the right decision for a leader to make."

Andrew was quiet for what felt like forever. It was at least a few solid minutes, and no one said a word. Then:

"Okay."

You could almost feel a sigh of relief from our entire team, Andrew included. It was like a weight was lifted now that the path was becoming clear.

"You're right. The movement is more important than anything. We can't throw it away. If dropping out makes it more likely that these ideas will remain popular and be taken seriously, if it will bring them closer to becoming a reality, it's the right call.

"BUT," he stressed, continuing. "This is a contingency plan. I still want us to play to win in New Hampshire. If we don't crack the top five, we'll skip the death march and drop out that night."

We looked at each other, somber. I nodded.

"Understood."

A couple of days later, I was backstage with Andrew at the McIntyre-Shaheen 100 Club Dinner. This was the largest event for New Hampshire Democrats in the entire primary cycle, held the Saturday before election night, and Manchester's Southern New Hampshire University Arena was mobbed. It was a packed stadium of ten thousand screaming Democrats, all waving signs and absolutely covered in candidate merch. And, frankly, they were pretty hostile. Fresh off the contested Iowa results, Pete and Bernie supporters were openly booing each other's candidates. In fact, when any candidate finished speaking, only that candidate's supporters would stand up or often even applaud at all. The rest would stay seated, as if in protest.

"Careful out there. It's an aggressive crowd," I warned Andrew as he was warming up backstage.

He poked his head out into the walkway where he could see Joe Biden wrapping up his speech. Even Joe had gotten some awkward silences from this audience, and he finished to one of the weaker ovations.

Andrew looked back at me and smiled.

"I got this," he said, and did his awkward dad jog onto the stage.

That night, Andrew delivered, in my opinion, his most complete performance as a candidate—all the confidence and swagger of a Yang Gang rally, coupled with all the humanity of his "Kids Are Not All Right" speech in November. When it ended, supporters of Sanders, Warren, Buttigieg, Biden, Klobuchar—all were on their feet, cheering for Andrew. It was, overwhelmingly, the most positive response that any candidate received, and seemingly the only point in the entire event when the whole party united in genuine applause. The speech felt like an exclamation point on his presidential run. And the massive standing ovation?

Frankly, it felt like a thank-you. *Thanks for running, Andrew Yang.*

And for the fourth time on the campaign, I cried like a baby. (Well, maybe not like a baby. But tears were shed.)

Three days later, Andrew finished in eighth place in the New Hampshire primary. That night, he officially dropped out of the race at the same restaurant we'd visited on our very first trip to New Hampshire: Puritan Backroom. I naturally drowned my emotions in their famous chicken fingers and White Russians, for old times' sake.

The night Andrew Yang dropped out, he received a huge outpouring of positive press—easily the most positive coverage of his entire campaign. It was amazing and shocking at the same time: media outlets, elected officials, pundits, and experts who had refused to acknowledge our existence all sang our praises! Heck, Bernie Sanders even said something nice about Andrew, something he hadn't done publicly even once over the course of the campaign.

Along with the public support, Andrew received calls from nearly every candidate, from a number of world leaders, and from some of the most influential people on both sides of the aisle. For those of us behind the scenes, it was a surreal series of incredible moments, a flood of glowing news and support as the world seemingly embraced Andrew Yang overnight, discussing the impact of his run, what it meant, and how his ideas might move the country in a positive direction. It was as if now that he was no longer a threat to the status quo, it was safe for the mainstream media to endorse Andrew Yang, to recognize him, rightfully, as one of the most influential figures in the race.

Our decision to define our collective success on our own terms was the right one. Now don't get me wrong: I'm not one for participation trophies or confusing effort with results. We freaking lost. That sucked. But this man, who could so easily have been just a blip on the American political radar, changed an entire nation's conversation around universal basic income and built a movement that millions nationwide identified with, and because we focused on defining our collective success and prioritized that movement, it didn't disappear when we dropped out. In fact, the flood of positivity and press after New Hampshire was just the beginning. Ideas and policies that had once been considered "fringe" when our campaign began started to gain widespread acceptance and approval. In the course of a little over a year after Andrew Yang exited the presidential primary, the following occurred:

- Due to the impacts of COVID-19 on the global economy, many of the worrisome trends and conditions that caused Andrew to run for president accelerated and became suddenly more recognized and discussed, including the automation of our most common jobs, the potential for civil unrest and violence, and widespread economic insecurity.
- During this crisis, governments around the world turned to the idea of direct cash relief to citizens. I've discussed this elsewhere in the book: public support came from across the political spectrum—you won't find much that Mitt Romney, Donald Trump, Nancy Pelosi, and even the pope all agree on, but they agreed on this.
- A new press narrative emerged, emphasizing Andrew's vision and influence and yielding the following headlines:

  "What if Andrew Yang was right?" (*The Atlantic*[7])

  "Is the Trump Administration Embracing Andrew Yang's Universal Basic Income?" (*USA Today*[8])

  "'My phone is blowing up,' Andrew Yang says as federal officials explore cash payouts to Americans" (*Los Angeles Times*[9])

  "Andrew Yang has spoken with Trump officials about a plan to directly give Americans cash to counter the coronavirus slump" (Business Insider[10])

"'I'll Be a Very Happy Man.' Will the Coronavirus Outbreak Turn Andrew Yang's $1,000 Promise Into Reality?" (*Time*[11])

"What Donald Trump, Bernie Sanders and Andrew Yang agree on: Giving out cash—now." (*San Francisco Chronicle*[12])

- The United States government distributed cash relief directly to the people, starting with $600 checks to individuals, and eventually passing legislation to send additional $1,200 and $1,400 checks to American adults in early 2021.

- Andrew and a few members of our campaign leadership team launched a new organization, Humanity Forward, to continue the movement we started. The organization was instrumental in lobbying Congress to include stimulus checks and various forms of direct cash relief in COVID-relief legislation, and it even gave millions in direct cash relief to thousands of Americans impacted by the pandemic—before the US government was able to pass any stimulus or aid legislation itself.

- Aside from COVID relief, pilot programs and/or versions of Andrew's universal basic income proposal have been implemented in dozens of cities around the United States, including Oakland (CA), Los Angeles, Denver, Gainesville (FL), Atlanta, Chicago, Gary (IN), Boston, St. Paul (MN), Jackson (MI), Newark, Pittsburgh, Columbia (SC), and Richmond (VA).[13]

- UBI gained mainstream momentum worldwide. More than 130 countries have now piloted direct cash transfer programs, including Canada, Brazil, Germany, Spain, the Netherlands, India, China, and Japan.[14]

- In March 2021, President Joe Biden signed into law an enhanced child tax credit providing families up to $3,600 for children under age six, and up to $3,000 for children between ages six and seventeen, with payments made directly to families monthly in installments of $300 or $250 per child. Many believe this is the official groundwork for a truly universal basic income in the United States.[15]

You might argue that, if not for the pandemic, Andrew's ideas wouldn't have gained the traction they did. And while it is true that the moment plays a role in the success of everything—every idea, every venture, every organization—it's also subject to forces beyond our control. In the final chapter, I'll talk more about this, about how it relates to identity branding, and more specifically about what I believe this all means for the future of politics (and for this movement).

But here, at the end of the story of our ridiculous, longer-than-longshot presidential campaign, I want to take a moment to reflect not on the future, but on what is undeniable about what we have already achieved. Andrew Yang changed the game for politicians and campaigns. At the beginning of this book, I said that Andrew Yang didn't just run for president—he built a brand and a movement. And this movement, created by an inexperienced candidate and a team of political nobodies, took its vision and ideas from the fringe to the popular majority with extraordinary speed, laying the groundwork to truly rewrite the rules of the American economy.

Whatever opinion you have about Andrew Yang, me, or our campaign, it is difficult to argue with the fact that this movement didn't just change the game. It changed the world.

9

THE BRAND FOR THE MOMENT
How Identity Branding Will Shape Our Future

I am so thrilled to announce that I am running for mayor of
New York City!

                                        —Andrew Yang, January 2021

AFTER ALL THE DROPOUT SPEECH HOOPLA AND SUPPORTIVE CALLS FROM FAMOUS people on election night in New Hampshire—but well before we could witness the wider impact of our campaign and movement—Evelyn, Andrew, and I piled into the back of an SUV to head to our hotel for our last night on the campaign trail before flying home to New York City. I sat in the back of the car, in the dark, in exhausted silence with the Yang family.

We were all thinking the same thing.

So . . . now what?

As it turned out, we didn't have long to ponder this. Within a month, the world had been turned upside down by the coronavirus pandemic. The energy we'd been pouring into the campaign had a sudden and urgent new direction, as we immediately worked to start the nonprofit Humanity Forward within a few short weeks—to advocate for cash relief and lobby Congress to pass effective aid that would directly support the people hurt the most by our economy shutting down. What's more, there was still an election underway, and Andrew was a main surrogate for Joe Biden in a number of swing states and even spoke at the Democratic National Convention. In November 2020, after Biden had won but the fate of the Senate still depended on a special runoff election in Georgia, Andrew moved his entire family down to Atlanta to help get out the vote, living there and helping grassroots organizers on the ground for over six weeks. When the runoff election happened in January 2021, the state saw record voter turnout, doubling the number of voters from the last Georgia runoff and seeing some of the biggest increases among Asian Americans.[1] In the end, the massive get-out-the-vote efforts by Democrats throughout the state flipped the traditionally red Georgia blue, helping deliver both the presidency and two new Senate seats.[2]

And a week before inauguration, on January 14, 2021, I found myself standing outside in the freezing cold, watching Andrew Yang declare his candidacy for mayor of New York City.

This is exciting! I remember thinking. *In the heart of the coronavirus pandemic, perhaps we can use our movement to save the city that Andrew and I call home.*

Andrew's entry into the NYC mayor's race felt like a way to continue what he had started on the presidential campaign trail; applying his ideas in the country's largest major city was a way to lead the nation forward. He entered the mayoral race as the most well-liked and well-known candidate in the entire field, riding the strong identity brand we'd built during his presidential run, a brand that had only become stronger since. Time, national approval, and a prominent gig as a CNN analyst in 2020 had allowed Andrew's identity to finally level up in the eyes of Democratic voters and pundits. We wouldn't have to rely on the gimmicks and attention grabbers that we'd needed as a no-name presidential candidate in a crowded field—Andrew the mayoral candidate was a more polished and serious version of Andrew the presidential candidate, with a clear path to victory. The press unanimously considered him the front-runner and the candidate to beat, a complete 180 degrees from 2020.

Unfortunately, that 180 degrees didn't apply to the results.

I'm not going to end this book with a complete postmortem of Andrew's NYC mayoral bid. Frankly, I'm not sure I'd be the best person to write one, since I actually wasn't in charge this time around. Don't get me wrong, I did help him recruit initial talent and build a starting infrastructure to run a serious race, and I remained a close confidant and sounding board throughout, but in reality, I was pretty burnt out on politics following the presidential race (see literally any chapter prior to this for reasons). I love the marketing, branding, and problem-solving aspects of politics, but day-to-day campaign management is not a particularly deep passion of mine.

Instead, I had the dream title of "senior advisor," a bullshit label that consultants love to use because a "senior advisor" never loses, no matter what happens to the candidate. In my case, if Andrew won, I'd get to say, "My advice helped him become mayor of the greatest city in the world." If he lost, I'd get to say, exactly like I am right now, "Well, I really wasn't in charge of anything so you can't blame me."

Regardless, as a senior advisor, I had a front-row seat, and witnessing how Andrew's strong identity brand performed in a completely new political context gave me a few new insights to share as we bring this book to a close. While this playbook has focused on the benefits of building an identity brand, and how it can help longshots compete in the attention economy, I've also alluded to a few of the potential pitfalls of this kind of marketing. These pitfalls can be summarized simply: *Because identity branding requires you to stake out a strong, unique persona, it can hinder your ability to change and adapt.* This is true in all fields and industries, to an extent—once you go in one direction, it can be harder to change course—but in politics this is a heightened concern, both for politicians and for everyone who cares about the future of our democracy.

There are two main reasons that strong identity brands struggle to change and adapt:

1. Identity branding disincentivizes compromise.

As we outlined in chapter two, to build a strong identity brand you must lean in to your strengths and create a "like us" feeling for potential supporters to easily identify with, focus on finding a tribe that fits that identity, and authentically take these supporters along for the ride. The shortcut to doing this as a politician is to take strong, uncompromising stances, typically on issues that are emotionally charged for voters, and link your identity to those positions.

This is a major shift from the past. For decades, we've all generally identified with the party, not the candidate. Sure, we've always had varying degrees of Republicans and Democrats, and seen a few third-party candidates thrown in there, but generally speaking, the political contenders over the past century have been variations (some more dramatic than others) on one brand: politician!

You instinctively know what I'm talking about—smooth talking, well dressed, and able to articulate and sell the party line on any issue. This brand of "politician" has relied heavily on the Bud Light marketing treatment we discussed earlier and has been beaten into our brains. For years, traditional politicians generally tried to avoid tying themselves too strongly to any absolute policy stance, prioritizing their ability to adapt to the changing political environment and stay in office. We knew these candidates were "safe," but did we know what they stood for? Mostly, what they stood for was simply their political party's brand, not their own.

This is changing. The traditional brand of politician is struggling to stand out in today's attention economy. Those currently in power may be able to chameleon their way through elections when the moment allows it (more on this, and Joe Biden, shortly), but they are fast being replaced by a new breed of politician born from our world of clickbait headlines and the 24-7 fight for attention.

These new up-and-coming political personalities are creating strong identity brands, sometimes unintentionally, that let them stand out. Often you'll see them pick an issue, loudly signal their position, and commit to it unquestionably. From there, many of them use tactics right out of our playbook—targeting alternative press to find new audiences, building savvy social media operations, and relying on twenty-first-century gamechangers like celebrities and influencers and small-dollar donors over establishment support. We are now seeing congressional representatives from tiny districts build massive armies of passionate supporters nationwide, something previously unheard of for a politician early in his or her political career.

That said, these new personalities carving out brands to compete in this space are double-edged swords. Think about the names you typically see in the headlines—progressive candidates like Alexandria Ocasio-Cortez infuriate the right and inspire the left. Far-right candidates like Marjorie Taylor Greene do the reverse. We're seeing candidates with strong identity brands dominate our political discourse, from Ilhan Omar to Matt Gaetz to Rashida Tlaib to Lauren Boebert, each capturing our attention and either firing us up or pissing us off. Plenty has been written about how our two-party system, twenty-four-hour news cycle, and social media-dominated culture are making us more polarized politically. While identity brands make it easier to compete in this landscape, they are making that polarization worse, not better.

The success of this model has led candidates up and down the ballot to adopt it, and elected officials and candidates for positions from school board to president now routinely take strong stances on polarizing issues like defunding the police and teaching critical race theory in public schools—and then tie those postures to their personal identities. For them, it's a very simple first step toward building an identity brand—*Like us, you hate/love this controversial policy!* If there's a hot-button issue in the United States of America today, you can almost guarantee that identity brands will be built to include uncompromising positions on one side or the other.

I say "uncompromising," because strong identity brands are not built for compromise. You've authentically staked out who you are and what you stand for, and you've found and convinced supporters to join. Compromising any part of that risks blowing up what you've built. For an elected official, this would mean lower fundraising numbers, losing volunteers and organizers, and getting a primary challenger in your next election. Politicians who link specific policy positions to their identity brands don't have room for compromise on those positions, because they become part of their "like us" connection with supporters.

Bernie Sanders: *Like us, you want Medicare for all.*

Donald Trump: *Like us, you want to build a wall.*

Andrew Yang: *Like us, you want universal basic income.*

Can you imagine the reaction among his supporters if Sanders announced that he was voting for privatized health care? Or if Trump came out in favor of amnesty for illegal immigrants, or if Yang abandoned the idea of UBI?

Strong identity brands essentially create strong principles, and sticking to them and staying authentic is how you continue engaging your supporters and bringing them along for the ride. But principles are broader than the details of policy. The issues elected officials must navigate are nuanced and complex. Think about yourself: it is completely possible that your authentic views on an issue might evolve over time as you learn more, or new information comes to light. That kind of mental flexibility, in fact, is a sign of intelligence. It is unquestionably a good thing when people learn and evolve their opinions when they get new information. What's more, getting things done in a democracy often requires compromise. Anyone who has ever worked on a team knows this—from group projects in high school to sports to church committees to for-profit companies. Strong leaders work to find win-win solutions, to move an organization forward for the team's greater good. When politicians tie their identity brands to specific policy stances, they have no incentive—or room—to grow or to compromise even if they want to.

And therein lies the rub for our elected officials who have won elections using a strong identity brand. On one side of the scale, you have sticking to your identity brand, which leads you to more money, press, attention, and supporters. On the other, you have compromising your identity brand to pass legislation that can help solve some of our nation's problems, which leads to less money, bad press, less attention, and a loss of core die-hard supporters. The result? Everyone sticks to their guns, and as expected, a lot gets said, and very little gets done.

2. Identity branding limits your ability to react to external changes.

I use the word "limits" here intentionally. If you have a strong identity brand, you are always able to respond to the circumstances around you in a way that is authentic to the identity you've created. But what if your identity brand doesn't fit the moment around you? If your supporters have strongly identified with your brand in one direction, and the world goes in another, what do you do? You can seem tone-deaf and irrelevant if you stay your current course, but can look foolish and inauthentic if you change it.

The stronger your identity brand, the harder it can be to change directions when circumstances around you shift. We dove into this in chapter seven, and we even suggested that a good way to minimize this is to build a brand that fits where you ultimately want to end up, not just where you're headed in the short term.

But I also said that, to a large extent, this downside of identity branding is generally unavoidable. Authentic identity branding is typically required to stand out in today's attention economy, and better to be a successful, popular brand in a world that is starting to move away from you than an ignored, irrelevant brand in a world that is perfectly suited for you. The world changes, cultural winds shift, things go in and out of fashion, and certain moments will always reward some efforts and activities over others. The pandemic, for instance, was a great moment for Peloton at-home workouts and a terrible one for Equinox high-end in-person workouts. Ideally, organizations and companies with strong identity brands can ride out a shift in circumstances, authentically navigating the headwinds and waiting for the moment to change again—because it almost always will.

In politics, however, while you may be able to weather shifting circumstances over the course of a career, it is often the moment that decides elections. Of course this has always been the case to some degree, but as politicians become less "all purpose"—brands that can fit nearly any moment—and instead create strong, uncompromising identities for themselves, this becomes a much bigger issue. Election cycles are often too short to allow for change in response to a shifting moment in our culture or the electorate, which means that whether or not you succeed depends more than ever on a factor you cannot control.

Our past two presidential elections are great examples of how identity brands can and cannot evolve to meet the moment. Prior to the 2016 election, Bernie Sanders had been saying the same thing for nearly four decades. He built a brand over many years around progressive policies such as universal health care, labor rights, and wealth inequality, and being a senator from Vermont seemed like his ceiling. However, in the 2016 primary, his anti-establishment populism provided the perfect contrast for those on the left who felt Hillary Clinton represented the corrupt political establishment and were dissatisfied with her as a candidate. His organic identity brand perfectly fit the moment and catalyzed the current progressive movement. While he didn't win, his authentic campaign drastically outperformed initial expectations, and many argue he would have had a real chance at taking the primary if not for the Democratic party establishment.[3]

Flash forward four years to 2020, when Bernie ran a campaign very similar to his 2016 effort and remained authentic to his anti-establishment brand of progressive populism. At the same time, Joe Biden leaned into his brand—that of an experienced traditional politician who could return us to pre-Trump America: "Restore the Soul of America," "Build Back Better," and "You Know Joe" were some of his main calling cards.

Democratic voters were justifiably terrified of losing to Trump again. Unfortunately, this meant there was minimal appetite for risk from both Democrats and anti-Trump Republicans, and the safest, most moderate candidate had an advantage nationwide.[4] The moment favored Joe Biden; Bernie's identity brand did not fit the moment, and there was little he could do about it.

On the other side of the aisle, Donald Trump was subject to the same forces. In 2016, Trump entered the presidential primary having been in the public eye seemingly his whole life. Branded as a ruthless but successful businessman who always spoke his mind, he, like Bernie, ran as an anti-establishment candidate—but one playing to a drastically different audience. He was the "our government is a disaster, might as well give the outsider a shot" candidate, and he won the

Republican primary and then the general election in 2016 because his identity brand fit a moment when many Americans felt left behind. In 2020, however, the moment had changed due to a global coronavirus pandemic. Trump's identity brand as an outsider who will "Drain the Swamp" and blow up the system was substantially less effective when we all needed government systems to lead us out of a global pandemic.

A politician with a strong identity brand that doesn't fit the moment is in a "damned if you do, damned if you don't" situation. You can stick to your authentic identity and find yourself out of favor with the general zeitgeist but hopefully keeping most of your die-hard supporters, or you can try to adapt your brand to meet the moment, potentially gaining new supporters but seriously risking losing the core supporters who built you into existence in the first place.

Building an identity brand creates your lane. When dynamics around you shift, it is nearly impossible to change lanes quickly without crashing. And for politicians, this can be the difference between winning and losing an election.

———————

When looked at through the lens of these downsides of identity branding, Andrew Yang's rise and eventual fall in the NYC mayor's race is much easier to understand. What's more, it becomes a stark illustration of the second of these downsides in particular. His brand was so powerfully set in the minds of the public, thanks to the 2020 presidential election, that it was impossible to switch his focus when the moment called for it.

I know this sounds a bit ridiculous . . . *he lost because his brand was too strong?* But hear me out.

The 2021 Democratic primary for the NYC mayoral election needs to be viewed in two sections: pre-vaccine (January to April 2021) and post-vaccine (May to June 2021).

Let's start with pre-vaccine. At this time:

- The pandemic dominated the headlines, to the exclusion of almost everything else
- Unemployment was climbing[5]
- Thousands of businesses had closed, with no timeline for reopening
- Schools were closed and frustrated parents were struggling to find childcare or be forced out of work

- Hundreds of thousands of New Yorkers had left the city[6]
- It was winter, and with the pandemic raging, most voters were stuck inside their homes
- The top issues for NYC voters were COVID and economic recovery[7]
- Among these voters, cash relief, Andrew's signature policy, had 81 percent approval[8]

New York City was in the middle of a massive and unprecedented economic crisis, and Andrew Yang's identity brand fit that environment perfectly. Visionary, smart, nontraditional, solutions-focused, optimistic—Andrew's "like us" persona and economic message were assets in a political environment that centered on the economy and COVID recovery. Another core part of his identity was his status as a nontraditional candidate, and while this had been a weakness later in the presidential primary race, it was easily spun as a strength here: the city needed someone with big ideas for this unprecedented moment, and Andrew Yang was an entrepreneur who had pioneered the movement around cash relief.

He began the race as a front-runner, and he even got some key endorsements (for instance, Congressman Ritchie Torres) right out of the gate. After the initial excitement around his launch, the local political press and other candidates threw everything they had at him, claiming that his presidential campaign had created a toxic bro culture,[9] that he "charmed" (read: sucked up to) Republicans,[10] and criticizing him for spending time in his house outside the city during the pandemic[11]— most of all, they attacked his authenticity as a New Yorker, criticizing everything from his use of the term "bodega,"[12] to tweets about taking the train,[13] to what he ate for lunch.[14] But these press hits didn't matter, because Andrew could remain authentically on message. When his New York bona fides were questioned, Andrew responded with this:

> *Anyone who thinks that somehow my New York–ness is in question should just come and say it to my face, and they'll see how ridiculous it is. If your plan during a crisis is to try to segment and divide New Yorkers against each other, you're probably the wrong person to lead the city.[15]*

And after nearly two months of negative headlines, Andrew went up in the polls another ten points, solidifying a double-digit lead in mid-March.[16] He seemed unstoppable.

But once the vaccine rolled out in April 2021, the moment changed.

This was the reality in New York City, post-vaccine:

- More than 200 million Americans were vaccinated, giving a sense that the worst of COVID had passed[17]
- NYC seemed to be returning to life as businesses started to reopen and economic activity rebounded
- The combination of warmer weather and reopening businesses let people get out of their homes
- Tourists and residents returned to the city in large numbers[18]
- Schools began reopening, to the relief of millions of parents
- Unemployment, while still high, dropped from its pandemic levels as companies started rehiring workers they'd laid off[19]
- Cash relief, Andrew's signature policy, was out of the news and no longer the top concern of voters[20]
- The city saw a massive spike in violent crime in all five boroughs, and shootings dominated the headlines (most notably, a four-year-old was shot in Times Square in broad daylight)[21]
- Crime and safety became NYC voters' top priority[22]

Andrew had built a strong brand around cash relief and forward-thinking economic ideas. When the race moved to crime, his message rapidly felt more and more out of place. In this new environment, not only did his core strengths become less powerful, some became weaknesses. His business background was an asset in an economic crisis, and the brand of "cash relief–focused outsider with big ideas" was perfect for a city concentrating on recovery. But in a city concerned with law and order, that outsider status became a liability: *What does a business-man know about crime? We need an experienced government leader to protect us!* The priority of public safety gave an advantage to traditional political gatekeepers like unions and Democratic clubs, who had ample experience promoting candidates with a tough-on-crime message.

By May 2021, less than eight weeks before the election, the brand that we had worked so hard to build during the presidential race—and which had seemed primed to save NYC's struggling economy during the COVID crisis—had become ineffective in the changed context of the (seemingly) "post-COVID" mayoral election that now centered around crime. And the polls quickly started to reflect that new reality.[23]

When this happened, Andrew had the same choice I outlined earlier—the choice that all strong identity brands have when it comes to compromising or adapting to a changing environment. He could stick to his original messaging, likely seeming tone-deaf and losing as a result but remaining authentic to his brand, or he could try to evolve to meet the moment, giving himself a better chance to win but compromising his authenticity. In this case, Andrew decided to meet the moment and shift his message, focusing on the need for a change in leadership to address public safety concerns and keep New York City safe. It was a play-to-win strategy, which I'll always respect, and it wasn't a total flop—he even managed to get endorsed by the firefighters' union and the police captains' union. But it never quite landed. When the race was all about the economy, it was easy for Andrew to be authentic. But public safety wasn't why he entered the race, and when he talked about it, not only did it feel inauthentic, it drew attention to his lack of experience on the issue. Andrew continued to drop in the polls, eventually finishing in fourth place behind three candidates with government experience and a stronger message for the moment.

In the end, Andrew Yang's strong identity brand was the mayoral campaign's downfall. No, he didn't run a perfect race. Anyone can point to certain tweets, quotes, press conferences, and unpolished moments on the trail (which the press eagerly hammered him for at every turn). But those are micro issues. His competitors in the mayoral race all had plenty of slipups themselves, and we had plenty on the presidential campaign as well. You can generally overcome those small hiccups in the attention economy, given our short attention spans. But you can't overcome not being the right brand for the moment.

So . . . what does this mean for politics going forward?

Simply put: everything.

This right here is actually the entire point of this book. Andrew Yang was just the beginning. Identity brands are the future. The industries that will continue to be taken over by them will see massive changes—and likely none more so than politics. If strong identity brands disincentivize compromise and limit the ability to adapt to a moment, and an effective politician needs to be able to compromise and adapt to electoral shifts during the tight timescales of an election, then this will have fascinating implications for the future of the United States of America.

For starters, I believe the Joe Biden brand of politician is slowly dying. Plain vanilla, Bud Light politicians, those with catch-all stances, who stand for everything so that in the end they stand for nothing but the party line—politicians like this will become less and less common in the attention economy. The traditional politician brand will still find some success, especially when there isn't a more authentic candidate to fit the moment, as they can draw on their chameleonlike ability to pivot to whatever message voters identify with at that time. But as time goes on and politicians with strong identity brands become more numerous and normalized, this will become less the rule and more the exception.

Instead, I predict that it will become harder and harder to win elections without strong stances and authentic identity branding. Our short attention spans and information saturation demand that you stand for something—those who don't will struggle to stand out. But if authenticity is going to rule the day, then the ability of our politicians to pivot quickly based on the political climate will drastically decrease. Which means political success will be less about your ability to inspire and smooth talk your way through press conferences and more about how your core identity matches the current political climate.

Crime is up? Candidates with an authentic identity brand on safety and violence will win the day.

The economy in shambles? Candidates who are authentically focused on the economy and business will thrive.

Racial justice at the center of the race? Candidates with authentic messages about identity and race will outperform.

We have already started to see politics increasingly shaped by candidates who have the right identity brand for the moment. Eric Adams branded himself strongly as a Black cop who was tough on crime. Supporters identified with his blue-collar résumé, his experiences as a Black man, and his strong stances on crime and gun violence—and he won the NYC mayoral primary and then the general election in decisive fashion. With crime as New York City's top issue, he had the brand the moment called for. But if his reelection campaign has to adapt to a different moment—like a failing economy, rising health-care costs, or attracting tourists— he may have a tough time pivoting and could be vulnerable to a challenger with a strong brand that is more on message in the moment.

We should expect to see congressional seats more hotly contested, with more shocking upsets, rapid rises to political power, and closer-than-expected races from once anonymous challengers. Incumbents will see their seats of power threatened, not because of their track record or a challenger who is particularly well funded, but because an establishment candidate might be the wrong brand for the moment.

Unfortunately, this likely means we'll be more divided and politics more divisive than ever. We can anticipate identity-branded candidates to prioritize the uncompromising stances that got them elected over the solving of actual problems, and plenty of food fights along the way.

———

The last takeaway I'll leave you with is that while this book has guided us through Andrew Yang's rise from longshot to national figure, the lessons here are about so much more than Andrew Yang.

Andrew Yang's 2020 presidential campaign proved that the game had changed. It rewrote the playbook for how to build an identity brand and use it to compete in today's attention economy. The playbook we used to take him from anonymous to contender will be adopted and adjusted across politics and by businesses for years to come. His performance in the presidential race proved that anyone can run for office and compete at the highest level. The implications of what this means for the future of politics, and beyond, have only just begun to take shape.

At the same time, Andrew Yang's 2021 campaign for mayor of New York City proved the downsides of identity branding's takeover of our political system, demonstrating that a strong identity brand can't simply pivot to a new message when the moment changes. The political leaders who rise to power over the next few decades will have increasingly less incentive to compromise and adapt. We can only imagine how this will impact our public discourse for years to come.

And as for Andrew Yang himself?

I'm pretty sure Andrew's legacy is still being written. For now, many will credit Andrew for championing universal basic income and moving certain ideas and policies into our national discourse and reality.

But I believe over time, he'll also be remembered for blazing a new trail. Andrew Yang's run proved that even a longer-than-longshot can become a contender, and it will give rise to a generation of future politicians, personalities, brands, and organizations who are looking to play by a new set of rules, the same way he did.

And from that standpoint, this longshot is just getting started.

ACKNOWLEDGMENTS

I OWE A LOT OF PEOPLE A GREAT DEAL OF THANKS FOR MAKING BOTH THIS BOOK and this movement happen.

Thank you to my editors, Alexa Stevenson and Alyn Wallace, for putting up with me and making me a better writer. Thank you to the entire BenBella team for believing in the vision of this book.

Thank you to Dave Larabell, Justin Edbrooke, Ari Levin and the CAA team, for allowing me to become a first-time author.

Thank you to the original Yang 2020 team—Andrew Frawley, Muhan Zhang, Matt Shinners—I hope this book serves as a fun reminder of the ridiculous and remarkable journey we shared.

Thank you to the initial Humanity Forward team—Ethan Dunn, Shelby Summerfield, Jon Lou, Conrad Taylor, and Ericka McLeod—for always having my back, deserved or not.

Thank you to the best debate prep team we could have asked for: Edward Chapman, Michael Hoeppner, and Aly Letsky.

Thank you to the Yang2020 team members who had to tolerate me the most—Liam deClive-Lowe, Katie Dolan, Luke Hansen, Madalin Sammons, Jonathan Herzog, Steve Marchand, Khrystina Snell, Al Womble, Jermaine Johnson, Haitao Wu, Nancy McDonald, Wendy Hamilton, Jeremy Frindel, Don Sun, Patricia Nelson, Kayle Jellesma, Haley Maiden, Justina Sullivan, Julian Low, Brea Baker, Dylan Enright, Heidi Day, Shaun Looney, Nick Ryan, Zach Fang, Heidi Day, Brian Yang, Lacey Delayne Hunt, Avery Kim, Edie Conekin-Tooze, Alex Damianou, Zack Guffey, Tvisha Dola, Jeff Kurzon, Mark Schmitz, Esther Baldwin, Eli Susser, Jacob Barr, Hilary Kinney, Heidi Johnson, Louisa Abel, Simon

Tam, Wesley Leung, Michael McDonagh, Ryan Ochoa, and the best bus driver ever, Puddin'.

Thank you to Erick Sanchez and Randy Jones for always providing me with Go-Go Juice on the campaign trail.

Thank you to the Yang Gang—to every single employee, volunteer, event attendee, and believer in this campaign. To all of the early event hosts who believed in us when no one would (you are the unsung heroes of this movement and we are forever grateful). To everyone who liked, watched, commented, and/or shared an Andrew Yang video. And countless others. You made this movement, and book, happen.

To everyone with a platform who supported our movement, and every reporter who gave us a fair shake when many others would not, including Elon Musk, Dave Chappelle, Donald Glover, Joe Rogan, Sam Harris, Teri Hatcher, Ben Shapiro, Bill Maher, Bari Weiss, Preet Bharara, Stephen Dubner, Scott Galloway, Chance the Rapper, Charlamagne tha God, Stephen Colbert, Ray Dalio, Ethan and Hila Klein, Kara Swisher, Tim Alberta, Liz Plank, Edward Isaac-Dover, Zach Montellaro, Chris Cillizza, Alex Thompson, Nancy Scola, Michael Kruse, MC Jin, Martin Luther King III, Wes Yang, Ben Smith, Cat Clifford, Cam Kasky, Elex Michaelson, Katy Tur, Chris Hayes, Stephanie Ruhle, Ali Velshi, Erin Burnett, Neil Cavuto, Brett Baier, Dave Weigel, Ruby Cramer, Holly Bailey, and Dan Merica.

Thank you to all the Yang-beat reporters who kept things interesting on the road—Julia Jester, Zohreen Shah, Nicole Sganga, Eugene Daniels, Brittany Shepherd, Jake Lahut, Amanda Golden, Armando Garcia, Alexandra Rego, Ben Mitchell, and Matt Stevens.

Thanks to my CNN friends who helped us tell Evelyn's story with grace and accuracy—Dana Bash, Bridget Nolan, Catherine Carter, Mark Preston, and Van Jones.

Thank you to the original Universal Basic Income champions who helped shape our campaign—Scott Santens and Andy Stern.

Thank you to Lauren Reilly and my SuitUp family. Your work, and the kids we help, inspire me to fight harder every day.

Thank you to my mentors at UBS—David McWilliams and John Amore. You encouraged me to jump—and caught me a few times when I didn't land so smoothly.

Thank you, Angie Elizalde, for keeping Andrew's and my hair on point.

Thank you, JJ and Kelly Keitzer, for believing in me.

Thank you, Evelyn Yang, for being a co-campaign manager when needed, and one of the bravest people I've ever met.

Thank you to my parents, for teaching me right and wrong, always having my back, praying for me every day, and not thinking I was too crazy when I joined the Yang campaign.

Thank you to my sister Tori for never hesitating to keep me grounded.

Thank you, Andrew Yang. You taught me to believe in a better future—and how to build one.

Thank you, Carly, the love of my life. As amazing as the campaign was, you were, and are, the best part.

And, last but not least, thank you to my brother, Jordan. The first official member of the Yang Gang. If you hadn't lit a fire under me, none of this would have happened.

ENDNOTES

Introduction

1. Zach Montellaro, "Andrew Yang raises $10 million in third quarter," *Politico*, October 2, 2019, https://www.politico.com/news/2019/10/02/andrew-yang-10-million-third-quarter-017382.
2. Gabriela Schlute, "Poll: Majority of voters now say the government should have a universal basic income program," *The Hill*, August 14, 2020, https://thehill.com/hilltv/what-americas-thinking/512099-poll-majority-of-voters-now-say-the-government-should-have-a.
3. "The most popular politicians in America," YouGov, Ongoing poll, https://today.yougov.com/ratings/politics/popularity/politicians/all.
4. Jada Yuan, "The surprising, enduring relevance of Andrew Yang and his ideas," *Washington Post*, March 23, 2020, https://www.washingtonpost.com/lifestyle/the-surprising-enduring-relevance-of-andrew-yang-and-his-ideas/2020/03/22/89a9d424-6ac3-11ea-b313-df458622c2cc_story.html.
5. Carmen Reinicke, "The first child tax credit payments go out to 65 million kids this week. How to navigate the process," CNBC, July 13, 2021, https://www.cnbc.com/2021/07/13/the-first-child-tax-credit-payments-go-out-this-week-what-to-know.html.

Chapter 1

1. Anu Narayanswamy, Darla Cameron, Matea Gold, "Election 2016: How much money is behind each campaign?" *Washington Post*, February 1, 2017, https://www.washingtonpost.com/graphics/politics/2016-election/campaign-finance/.

2. Daniel Levitin, "Why It's So Hard To Pay Attention, Explained By Science," *Fast Company*, September 23, 2015, https://www.fastcompany.com/3051417/why-its-so -hard-to-pay-attention-explained-by-science.

3. Bernard Marr, "How Much Data Do We Create Every Day? The Mind-Blowing Stats Everyone Should Read," *Forbes*, May 21, 2018, https://www.forbes.com/sites /bernardmarr/2018/05/21/how-much-data-do-we-create-every-day-the-mind -blowing-stats-everyone-should-read/?sh=6173e6e860ba.

4. Paul McDougall, "Humans Can Only Think About Four Things At Once, Study Says," Information Week, January 29, 2008, https://www.informationweek.com /it-life/humans-can-only-think-about-four-things-at-once-study-says.

Chapter 2

1. Natalie Coleman, "Basic Income Recipients Spent the Money on 'Literal Necessities,'" Futurism, October 4, 2019, https://futurism.com/basic-income-money-spent -necessities.

Chapter 3

1. "Joe Rogan Experience #1245—Andrew Yang," YouTube video, 1:52:02, posted by PowerfulJRE, February 12, 2019, https://www.youtube.com/watch?v=cTsEzm FamZ8.

2. Fundraising information sourced from Friends of Andrew Yang private ActBlue pages.

3. Rock Toaster, Twitter Post, February 24, 2019, https://twitter.com/RockToaster /status/1099820444733980673?s=20.

4. Jason Lemon, "Over 40% Of Andrew Yang Supporters Refuse To Support A Democratic Nominee That Isn't Him, Poll Shows," *Newsweek*, February 3, 2020, https:// www.newsweek.com/over-40-andrew-yang-supporters-refuse-support-democratic -nominee-that-isnt-him-poll-shows-1485458.

5. David Wright, "Andrew Yang raises $1.7 million for 2020 bid in first quarter," CNN, April 2, 2019, https://www.cnn.com/2019/04/02/politics/andrew-yang-first -quarter-fundraising-announcement/index.html.

Chapter 4

1. Stephen Covey Quotes, BrainyQuote.com, BrainyMedia Inc, 2021, https://www .brainyquote.com/quotes/stephen_covey_110198, accessed October 2, 2021.

2. Rebecca Morin, "Julián Castro on 2020 presidential run: 'I'm likely to do it,'" *Politico*, October 16, 2018, https://www.politico.com/story/2018/10/16/julian-castro -2020-presidential-run-907333.

3. "List of registered 2020 presidential candidates," *Ballotpedia*, November 3, 2020, https://ballotpedia.org/List_of_registered_2020_presidential_candidates.

4. Perry Bacon Jr, "Who's Behaving Like A 2020 Presidential Candidate," FiveThirty-Eight, October 11, 2018, https://fivethirtyeight.com/features/whos-behaving-like-a-2020-presidential-candidate/.

5. "DNC Announces Details For The First Two Presidential Primary Debates," Democratics.org, February 14, 2019, https://democrats.org/news/dnc-announces-details-for-the-first-two-presidential-primary-debates/.

6. Sam Stein, "How Little Known Andrew Yang May End Up on the 2020 Debate Stage by Gaming the System," Daily Beast, March 7, 2019, https://www.thedailybeast.com/how-little-known-andrew-yang-may-end-up-on-the-2020-debate-stage-by-gaming-the-system.

7. Dennis Silverman, "Campaign Finance: The Large and the Small," *Southern California Energy Blog*, January 26, 2020, https://sites.uci.edu/energyobserver/2020/01/26/campaign-finance-the-large-and-the-small/.

8. Fundraising information sourced from Friends of Andrew Yang private ActBlue pages.

Chapter 5

1. Troy Patterson, "Democratic Debate 2019: Andrew Yang's Bold Lack of a Tie," *New Yorker*, June 27, 2019, https://www.newyorker.com/news/current/democratic-debate-2019-andrew-yangs-bold-lack-of-a-tie.

2. Ashley Collman, "Andrew Yang went for a casual look at the Democratic debate, leading Brian Williams to ask 'Would it kill you to throw on a tie?'" Business Insider, June 27, 2019, https://www.businessinsider.com/andrew-yang-did-not-wear-tie-to-democratic-debate-2019-6.

3. Díamaris Martino, "Presidential hopeful Andrew Yang's 'missing tie' has its own Twitter account now," CNBC, June 28, 2019, https://www.cnbc.com/2019/06/28/andrew-yangs-missing-tie-has-its-own-twitter-account-now.html.

4. Hope Schreiber, "Andrew Yang appears without a tie during Democratic debate, and people have some feelings," Yahoo!, June 27, 2019, https://www.yahoo.com/lifestyle/andrew-yang-appears-without-a-tie-during-democratic-debate-and-people-have-some-feelings-014629722.html.

5. Ledyard King and John Fritze, "Andrew Yang goes (GASP!) tie-less on Democratic debate stage," *USA Today*, June 27, 2019, https://www.usatoday.com/story/news/politics/elections/2019/06/27/democratic-debate-2019-andrew-yang-scraps-tie-casual-look/1591330001/.

Chapter 6

1. "Democratic Presidential Nomination," RCP Polling Average, Real Clear Politics, September 10, 2019, https://www.realclearpolitics.com/epolls/2020/president/us/2020_democratic_presidential_nomination-6730.html#polls.

2. P.R. Lockhart, "Joe Biden's record on school desegregation busing, explained," Vox, July 16, 2019, https://www.vox.com/policy-and-politics/2019/6/28/18965923/joe-biden-school-desegregation-busing-democratic-primary.

3. Christopher Brito, "Kamala Harris' 2020 campaign now selling 'That Little Girl Was Me' T-shirts following viral exchange with Joe Biden," CBS News, June 28, 2019, https://www.cbsnews.com/news/kamala-harris-debate-joe-biden-t-shirts-that-little-girl-was-me-racial-segregation/.

4. Matt Stevens, "Kamala Harris Surges in 3 Polls After Strong Debate Performance," *New York Times*, July 2, 2019, https://www.nytimes.com/2019/07/02/us/politics/kamala-harris-polls.html.

5. Sam Stein, Twitter post, September 11, 2019, https://twitter.com/samstein/status/1171848261717635078?s=20.

6. r/YangForPresidentHQ, "I disliked the giveaway until they laughed," September 12, 2019, https://www.reddit.com/r/YangForPresidentHQ/comments/d3h31z/i_disliked_yangs_giveaway_until_they_laughed/.

7. Fundraising information sourced from Friends of Andrew Yang private ActBlue pages.

8. Alex Thompson, "Andrew Yang's campaign says over 450,000 people have entered debate contest," *Politico*, September 16, 2019, https://www.politico.com/story/2019/09/16/andrew-yang-campaign-debate-lottery-1497649.

9. r/YangForPresidentHQ, "Did the giveaway work? Andrew Yang most searched candidate during the debates," Reddit, September 12, 2019, https://www.reddit.com/r/YangForPresidentHQ/comments/d3j24a/did_the_giveaway_work_andrew_yang_most_searched/.

10. Dan Diamond (*Washington Post* reporter), Twitter post, Sept. 12, 2019, https://twitter.com/ddiamond/status/1172341494780321795?s=20.

11. Zach Graumann, Twitter post, September 16, 2019, https://twitter.com/Zach_Graumann/status/1173561504110714881?s=20.

12. MTV News Staff, "Andrew Yang Announces $120,000 Contest at Democratic Primary Debate," MTV, September 12, 2019, http://www.mtv.com/news/3138964/andrew-yang-democratic-primary-debate-contest/.

13. "Andrew Yang Kicks Off Democratic Debates With Promise of $120K Giveaway," *Hollywood Reporter*, September 12, 2019, https://www.hollywoodreporter.com/news/general-news/andrew-yang-kicks-democratic-debates-promise-120k-giveaway-1239340/.

14. Christopher Zara, "Here's how to enter Andrew Yang's universal basic income raffle giveaway," *Fast Company*, September 12, 2019, https://www.fastcompany.com/90403661/andrew-yang-ubi-money-giveaway-heres-how-to-enter-raffle.

15. Press mentions sourced from internal Friends of Andrew Yang media mention algorithms.

16. Megan Cerullo, "450,000 apply for shot at Andrew Yang's $1,000-a-month offer," CBS News, September 16, 2019, https://www.cbsnews.com/news/andrew-yang-online-raffle-450000-apply-for-one-of-2020-presidential-candidates-freedom-dividends-of-1000-a-month/.

17. Dan Merica, "Andrew Yang raises $10 million in third quarter, dwarfing previous hauls," CNN, October 2, 2019, https://www.cnn.com/2019/10/02/politics/yang-10-million-third-quarter/index.html.

18. "California 2020: Biden, Sanders, Warren in Statistical Tie in Democratic Primary; Harris Struggles in Home State," Emerson College Polling, September 16, 2019, https://emersonpolling.reportablenews.com/pr/california-2020-biden-sanders-warren-in-statistical-tie-in-democratic-primary-harris-struggles-in-home-state.

19. "Kamala Harris Drops Out of Presidential Race," NPR, December 3, 2019, https://www.npr.org/2019/12/03/784443227/kamala-harris-drops-out-of-presidential-race.

20. Dan Merica, "Andrew Yang raises $10 million in third quarter, dwarfing previous hauls," CNN, October 2, 2019, https://www.cnn.com/2019/10/02/politics/yang-10-million-third-quarter/index.html.

Interlude

1. Chris Cillizza, "Andrew Yang is the hottest 2020 candidate this side of Elizabeth Warren right now," CNN, September 12, 2019, https://www.cnn.com/2019/09/12/politics/andrew-yang-democrats-2020.

2. "Andrew Yang: Favorable/Unfavorable," RealClearPolitics, February 9, 2020, https://www.realclearpolitics.com/epolls/other/andrew_yang_favorableunfavorable-6840.html.

3. "Democratic Presidential Nomination" RCP Polling Average, RealClearPolitics, October 3, 2019, https://www.realclearpolitics.com/epolls/2020/president/us/2020_democratic_presidential_nomination-6730.html#polls.

4. "New Hampshire Democratic Primary Results," *USA Today*, February 27, 2020, https://www.usatoday.com/elections/results/primaries/democratic/new-hampshire/.

Chapter 7

1. "Democratic Presidential Candidate Polls," *Politico*, November 3, 2019, https://www.politico.com/2020-election/democratic-presidential-candidates/polls/.
2. Mark Benjamin, "It's 3 a.m. Who do you want answering the phone?" Salon, March 6, 2008, https://www.salon.com/2008/03/06/commander_in_chief_2/.
3. Mark Silva, "Obama turns Clinton's '3 a.m. call' ad back at her," *Chicago Tribune*, February 29, 2008, https://www.chicagotribune.com/chinews-mtblog-2008-02-obama_returns_fire_at_clintons-story.html.
4. Eliza Collins, Tarini Parti, "The Moments That Mattered at Iowa's Democratic Dinner," *Wall Street Journal*, November 2, 2019, https://www.wsj.com/articles/the-moments-that-mattered-at-iowas-democratic-dinner-11572698462.
5. Eric Bradner, Dan Merica, "7 takeaways from Iowa Democrats' biggest night of the year," CNN, November 2, 2019, https://www.cnn.com/2019/11/02/politics/iowa-democratic-dinner-takeaways/index.html.
6. Dominic Rushe, "Yang Gang: meet the fans of the 2020 hopeful who wants to give Americans $1,000 a month," *Guardian*, September 8, 2019, https://www.theguardian.com/us-news/2019/sep/07/andrew-yang-yang-gang-2020-freedom-dividends.
7. Rich Noyes, "Debate Host ABC News Has Ignored Most 2020 Democrats This Year," *MRC NewsBusters*, September 12, 2021, https://www.newsbusters.org/blogs/nb/rich-noyes/2019/09/12/debate-host-abc-news-has-ignored-most-2020-democrats-year.
8. Scott Santens, "A Visual History of the #YangMediaBlackout," Swamp, November 22, 2020, https://vocal.media/theSwamp/a-visual-history-of-the-yang-media-blackout.
9. Emily Stewart, "Donald Trump Rode $5 Billion in Free Media to the White House," The Street, November 20, 2016, https://www.thestreet.com/politics/donald-trump-rode-5-billion-in-free-media-to-the-white-house-13896916.
10. Meredith Conroy, "Why Being 'Anti-Media' Is Now Part Of The GOP Identity," FiveThirtyEight, April 5, 2021, https://fivethirtyeight.com/features/why-being-anti-media-is-now-part-of-the-gop-identity/.
11. Conroy, "Why Being 'Anti-Media' Is Now Part Of The GOP Identity."
12. Kevin Quealy, Quoctrung Bui, "Who Watched the Debates on Television, Minute By Minute," *New York Times*, October 23, 2020, https://www.nytimes.com/interactive/2020/10/23/upshot/debate-viewership-democrats-republicans.html.
13. "Democratic debate speaking time: By the numbers," CNN, November 20, 2019, https://www.cnn.com/2019/11/20/politics/dem-debate-speaking-time-november/index.html.
14. "November National Poll: Support for Impeachment Declines; Biden and Sanders Lead Democratic Primary," Emerson College Polling, November 20, 2019, https://emersonpolling.reportablenews.com/pr/november-national-poll-support-for-impeachment-declines-biden-and-sanders-lead-democratic-primary.

15. Polling information sourced from internal Friends of Andrew Yang polls that were not released publicly, created by Patinkin Research Strategies.

Chapter 8

1. David Axelrod, Twitter post, September 4, 2020, https://twitter.com/davidaxelrod /status/1301977756956229632.

2. Employee data sourced from Friends of Andrew Yang reporting through Gusto.

3. Sean Sullivan, "Bernie Sanders staffers complained about the campaign's use of Amazon, a frequent Sanders target," *Washington Post*, December 29, 2019, https:// www.washingtonpost.com/politics/bernie-sanders-staffers-complained-about-the -campaigns-use-of-amazon-a-frequent-sanders-target/2019/12/28/65b32350-265c -11ea-ad73-2fd294520e97_story.html.

4. Alex Thompson, "Women of color bolt Warren's Nevada campaign in frustration," *Politico*, February 6, 2020, https://www.politico.com/news/2020/02/06/elizabeth -warren-campaign-nevada-111595.

5. Bianca Padro Ocasio, "Biden's campaign is 'suppressing the Hispanic vote' in Flor- ida, an internal letter claims," *Miami Herald*, July 25, 2020, https://www.miami herald.com/news/politics-government/article244480437.html.

6. Reid Epstein, "How People of Color Inside the Buttigieg Campaign Sought to Be Heard," *New York Times*, January 28, 2020, https://www.nytimes.com/2020/01/28 /us/politics/buttigieg-campaign-black-hispanic-staff.html.

7. Jason Lemon, "Kamala Harris Campaign Accused of Treating Staff 'So Poorly' and Not Having 'a Real Plan to Win,'" *Newsweek*, November 29, 2019, https:// www.newsweek.com/kamala-harris-campaign-accused-treating-staff-so-poorly-not -having-real-plan-win-1474851.

8. Adam Harris, "What if Andrew Yang was right?" *The Atlantic*, March 16, 2020, https://www.theatlantic.com/politics/archive/2020/03/coronavirus-romney-yang -money/608134/.

9. Andrew Soergel, "Is the Trump Administration Embracing Andrew Yang's Uni- versal Basic Income?" *USA Today*, March 27, 2020, https://www.usnews.com/news /economy/articles/2020-03-27/shades-of-andrew-yangs-universal-basic-income -apparent-in-coronavirus-stimulus-checks.

10. Melissa Gomez, "'My phone is blowing up,' Andrew Yang says as federal officials explore cash payouts to Americans," *Los Angeles Times*, March 17, 2020, https://www.la times.com/politics/story/2020-03-17/andrew-yang-coronavirus-cash-payments-trump.

11. Grace Panetta, "Andrew Yang has spoken with Trump officials about a plan to directly give Americans cash to counter the coronavirus slump," Business Insider, March 17, 2020, https://www.businessinsider.com/andrew-yang-white-house-about -direct-cash-payment-plan-coronavirus-2020-3.

12. Abby Vesoulis, "'I'll Be a Very Happy Man.' Will the Coronavirus Outbreak Turn Andrew Yang's $1,000 Promise Into Reality?" *Time*, March 17, 2020, https://time.com/5804656/ubi-yang-coronavirus/.

13. Joe Garofoli, "What Donald Trump, Bernie Sanders and Andrew Yang agree on: Giving out cash—now," *San Francisco Chronicle*, March 19, 2020, https://www.sfchronicle.com/politics/article/What-Donald-Trump-Bernie-Sanders-and-Andrew-Yang-15141738.php.

14. Chase DiBenedetto, "Every U.S. city testing free money programs," Mashable, May 3, 2021, https://mashable.com/article/cities-with-universal-basic-income-guaranteed-income-programs.

15. Sigal Samuel, "Everywhere Universal Basic Income has been tried, in one map," Vox, October 20, 2020, https://www.vox.com/future-perfect/2020/2/19/21112570/universal-basic-income-ubi-map.

16. Carmen Reinicke, "The first child tax credit payments go out to 65 million kids this week. How to navigate the process," CNBC, July 13, 2021, https://www.cnbc.com/2021/07/13/the-first-child-tax-credit-payments-go-out-this-week-what-to-know.html.

Chapter 9

1. Nathaniel Rakich, Geoffrey Skelley, Laura Bronner, and Julia Wolfe, "How Democrats Won the Georgia Runoffs," FiveThirtyEight, January 7, 2021, https://fivethirtyeight.com/features/how-democrats-won-the-georgia-runoffs/.

2. Kimmy Yam, "Asian American voter rates in Georgia hit record high. How voting bill threatens progress," NBC News, March 31, 2021, https://www.nbcnews.com/news/asian-america/asian-american-voter-rates-georgia-hit-record-high-how-voting-n1262682.

3. Michael D. Shear and Matthew Rosenberg, "Released Emails Suggest the DNC Derided the Sanders Campaign," *New York Times*, July 22, 2016, https://www.nytimes.com/2016/07/23/us/politics/dnc-emails-sanders-clinton.html.

4. Matthew Sheffield, "Dem voters care more about beating Trump than any one policy issue," *The Hill*, May 17, 2019, https://thehill.com/hilltv/what-americas-thinking/444295-poll-democratic-voters-prioritize-defeating-trump-over-their.

5. Nick Reisman, "New York's Unemployment Rate Ticked Upward in January," Spectrum News, March 21, 2021, https://www.ny1.com/nyc/all-boroughs/ny-state-of-politics/2021/03/12/new-york-s-unemployment-rate-ticked-upward-in-january.

6. Jenna DeAngelis, "Over 333,000 New Yorkers Have Left City Since COVID Pandemic Began In March," CBS New York, January 8, 2021, https://newyork.cbslocal.com/2021/01/08/moving-out-of-nyc/.

7. Democrats for Education Reform NY, "ERNA NY Poll Shows Andrew Yang Leading in NYC Mayoral Race," December 21, 2020, https://dfer.org/ny/erna-ny-poll-shows-andrew-yang-leading-in-nyc-mayoral-race/.

8. Polling information sourced from internal Yang For New York polls that were not released publicly, created by Slingshot Strategies.

9. Editorial staff, "Andrew Yang's Presidential Campaign Had a 'Toxic' Bro Culture That Drove Women to Therapy, Report Says," Yahoo!, February 3, 2021, https://www.yahoo.com/now/andrew-yang-presidential-campaign-had-192856097.html.

10. Sally Goldenberg and Tina Nguyen, "How Andrew Yang charmed the right on his road to political stardom," *Politico*, March 15, 2021, https://www.politico.com/states/new-york/albany/story/2021/03/15/how-yang-charmed-the-right-on-his-road-to-political-stardom-1368366.

11. Katie Glueck, "Can Andrew Yang Make It in New York City Politics?" *New York Times*, January 12, 2021, https://www.nytimes.com/2021/01/11/nyregion/andrew-yang-mayor-nyc.html.

12. Chris Crowley, "Andrew Yang Walks Into a Bodega—or Does He?" *Grub Street*, January 15, 2021, https://www.grubstreet.com/2021/01/andrew-yang-bodega.html.

13. Clayton Guse, "NYC mayoral wannabe Andrew Yang appears to believe A train goes to the Bronx," *Daily News*, March 1, 2021, https://www.nydailynews.com/new-york/ny-andrew-yang-subway-a-train-bronx-20210301-bqbw7o3kbnbwzeukrfstig5f64-story.html.

14. Hannah Albertine, "Let's Overanalyze Andrew Yang's Instagram Meals," The Infatuation, February 17, 2021, https://www.theinfatuation.com/new-york/features/lets-overanalyze-andrew-yangs-instagram-meals.

15. Sabrina Franza, Twitter post, January 14, 2021, https://twitter.com/sabrinafranza/status/1349814474367246336?s=20.

16. Carl Campanile and Kenneth Garger, "Andrew Yang tops Democratic candidates for NYC mayor, poll finds," *New York Post*, March 9, 2021, https://nypost.com/2021/03/09/andrew-yang-tops-democratic-candidates-for-nyc-mayor-poll/.

17. Our World In Data, "Coronavirus (COVID-19) Vaccinations," as of July 14, 2021, https://ourworldindata.org/covid-vaccinations?country=USA.

18. Patrick McGeehan, "New York Is Reawakening. It Just Needs Its Tourists Back," *New York Times*, May 13, 2021, https://www.nytimes.com/2021/05/13/nyregion/nyc-tourism-covid.html.

19. Patrick McGeehan, "New York City Lost 900,000 Jobs. Here's How Many Have Come Back," *New York Times*, May 21, 2021, https://www.nytimes.com/2021/05/21/nyregion/unemployment-nyc-reopening-jobs.html.

20. Polling information sourced from internal Yang For New York polls that were not released publicly, created by Slingshot Strategies.

21. Magee Hickey, Stephen M. Lepore, Rebecca Solomon, "Police searching for suspect after 2 women, 4-year-old injured in Times Square shooting: officials," KXAN, May 8, 2021, https://www.kxan.com/news/times-square-on-lockdown-after-woman-child-injured-in-shooting-officials/.

22. Brigid Bergin, "Crime Is The Key Issue In New York City Mayor's Race," NPR, June 11, 2021, https://www.npr.org/2021/06/11/1005572002/crime-is-the-key-issue-in-new-york-city-mayors-race.

23. Henry Goldman and Skylar Woodhouse, "Andrew Yang Loses NYC Poll Lead as Rivals Stress Experience Gap," Bloomberg, May 26, 2021, https://www.bloomberg.com/news/articles/2021-05-26/yang-s-nyc-mayoral-quest-slips-as-foes-target-inexperience.

INDEX

ABOUT THE AUTHOR

"(Zach Graumann) hacked the primary with no political experience."
—Business Insider, February 29, 2020

ZACH GRAUMANN IS AN ENTREPRENEUR, POLITICAL OPERATIVE, AUTHOR, PODCAST host, marketing expert, and recovering Wall Street executive. Most notably, he was the Campaign Manager for Andrew Yang's 2020 presidential campaign, which he took from what was called *"a longer-than-long-shot"* (according to *The New York Times* in February 2018), to polling, nationwide, in the top five, having "hacked the primary" (*Business Insider* in 2020) in less than a year. Raising nearly $40 million dollars in an average of $35 increments, Yang2020 saw Andrew Yang in seven Democratic primary debates, outlasting four senators, four governors, seven members of Congress, two mayors, and one cabinet secretary. According to CNN, the campaign *"didn't just make history . . . [it] unquestionably put a sizable dent in the future as well."*

Zach is also the Co-Founder of two non-profit organizations: Humanity Forward, which has given millions of dollars in direct cash relief to Americans throughout the COVID-19 pandemic, and SuitUp, which brings companies into classrooms to increase career awareness and marketable skills for low-income students. To date, SuitUp has hosted hundreds of volunteer events nationwide with companies like Goldman Sachs, Conde Nast, NBCUniversal and LinkedIn, impacting more than 20,000 students and corporate volunteers across the country.

Prior to entering politics, Zach was the Head of Client Philanthropy Solutions at UBS Wealth Management Americas. He and his work have been featured in the *New York Times,* Business Insider, the *Washington Post, Rolling Stone, Politico,* CNN, Daily Beast, and *The Late Show with Stephen Colbert.*

Zach is a recipient of the Distinguished Alumni Award from his alma mater, Duke University, receiving a B.A. in Public Policy and a certificate in Markets and Management. He regularly speaks as an expert in innovative marketing, entrepreneurship, impact investing, and strategic philanthropy, and, with Andrew Yang, co-hosts *Forward,* a podcast. He currently resides in Manhattan and is passionate about education, entrepreneurship, corporate volunteering, woodworking, a cappella and the Buffalo Bills.